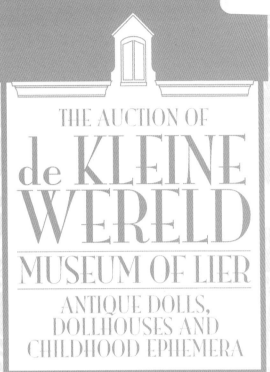

THE AUCTION OF de KLEINE WERELD MUSEUM OF LIER

ANTIQUE DOLLS, DOLLHOUSES AND CHILDHOOD EPHEMERA

"This is so nice about collecting: it is hard to say if you find a piece, or if the piece finds you. Mostly it is love at first sight."

Els Van Houtven, co-founder of De Kleine Wereld Museum

© Copyright 2012 Theriault's Gold Horse Publishing. All rights reserved.
No part of this book may be reproduced or utilized in any form or by any means, electronic or mechanical, including photocopying, recording, or by an information retrieval system, without permission, in writing, from the author or the publisher.

To order additional copies contact:
Dollmasters, PO Box 2319, Annapolis, MD 21404
Tel. 800-966-3655   Fax 410-571-9605
www.dollmasters.com

This book is based upon an antique collection auctioned by Theriault's of Annapolis, Maryland.

Design: Travis Hammond
Photography: Gerald Nelson

$59
ISBN: 1-931503-74-5
Printed in Hong Kong

It began with a tea cup.

Or, as Els Van Houtven of De Kleine Wereld Museum relates, "One day in 1976 we went antique shopping in Antwerp and we returned home with one small doll's cabinet with 3 drawers, painted salmon pink and missing one leg, and two pieces of a tea set that did not even belong together."

So began a 36 year quest for antique playthings of little girls. The collection eventually filled the large Liers, Belgian home of Lena de Swert, the mother of Els Van Houten, and led to the fulfillment of the mother and daughter dream, to create a museum for all to enjoy. A beautiful building in the historic Belgium village was chosen for De Kleine Wereld Museum and the dolls, doll furniture and doll houses were presented in breath-taking settings that earned the museum a reputation as one of the world's most beautiful doll and dollhouse museums.

1. Superb Early Parfumerie with Chandelier and Mirrors for the French Market

12" (30 cm.) h. x 18"l. x 9"d. The light-wood open-front shop has an unusual three-sided back and two side facades that give dimension and a sense of greater size to the tiny size. The walls, of cobalt blue paper, are decorated lavishly with gold paper borders and raised-construction gilt papers that suggest carving (especially notable on the side wall frames). There are two mirrors, and liberal floral and cherub decoupage. There are three curved-front shelves at the sides and back, and unusual stepped shelves at the sides of the front counter. An ormolu and glass chandelier hangs above, a porcelain lady doll stands in attendance, and the shop is fitted with glass and paper mache perfume and toiletry jars and bottles. The exterior has original old paper-covered surface. Excellent condition. For the French market, circa 1875. $1400/2100

2. Rare Early German Porcelain Doll in Original Costume

5" (13 cm.) Porcelain shoulder head with pink-tinted complexion, black sculpted hair in short uniform curls, painted features, muslin body, porcelain pink-tinted hands, porcelain painted knee-high boots on slender legs. Condition: generally excellent. Comments: Germany, circa 1865. Value Points: superb all-original condition, wearing original court costume in the 16th-century style including brass chest armor and various accessories. $300/600

3. French Cobalt Blue Sevres Miniature Glassware
3" (8 cm.) Of vibrant cobalt blue glass with hand-painted gold leaf rims and star designs, comprising carafe and shallow bowl. To perfectly display with 17"-21" lady dolls. French, the uniquely rich cobalt blue color was made famous in Sevres during the 18th century and thereafter, lending a special richness to porcelain, glassware, and even doll eyes of the mid-19th century. $200/400

4. French Porcelain Miniature Toilette Set on Dressing Table
6" (15 cm.) l. table. 4"h. 1 ¾"h. pitcher. A white porcelain wash set with blue and old decorations is arranged upon a wooden dressing table with bottom shelf and working drawer. The wash set includes wash bowl and pitcher, two lidded boxes, one open bowl, one lidded bowl. Excellent condition. French, circa 1875. $300/500

5. Petite French Bisque Poupée, Size 00, by Jumeau
10" (25 cm.) Bisque swivel head on kid-edged bisque shoulder plate, pale blue glass enamel inset eyes, dark eyeliner, lightly-feathered lashes and brows, accented nostrils, pierced ears, closed mouth with accented lips, pierced ears, blonde mohair wig over cork pate, shapely kid poupée body with gusset-jointing at hips, pretty antique gown, undergarments, fine bonnet. Condition: generally excellent, kid at right wrist weak. Marks: 00 (head) Jumeau Medaille d'Or Paris (body). Comments: Emile Jumeau, circa 1880. Value Points: most appealing gentle expression enhanced by very rare 00 petite size, original signed body, lovely bisque. $900/1300

6. French Porcelain Doll's Tea Set in Original Store Presentation Basket

12" (30 cm.) l. basket. 2 ½"h. teapot. The boat-shaped handled basket is filled with its porcelain doll's tea service with pink flower and blue rim decorations, comprising lidded teapot, lidded sugar, creamer, six cups and saucers, and six gilt metal spoons, each still tied into the basket with original red silk ribbons. Excellent condition. French, the charming arrangement likely appeared in French Etrennes catalogs of the era as a special store holiday gift, circa 1890. $300/500

7. French Miniature Blown Glass Carafe Set in Original Box

6 ½" (17 cm.) x 6 ½" box. 3 ½" carafe. A wooden box with lithographed-paper cover (curiously depicting kittens at play) with original gold lettering "Verre d'Eau" hinges open to fitted interior of blown glass crystal decorated with hand-painted gold leaf and floral designs, comprising round tray, two carafes with stoppers, two stemmed glasses, and a lidded jar. Excellent condition. French, circa 1885, rare and perfectly preserved doll-sized luxury accessory, for perfect display with poupées 17"-22". $400/600

#7 lid detail

8. French Cast Silver Miniature Vitrine with Depose Mark

8" (20 cm.) Of heavy cast metal with darkened silver finish, the miniature vitrine in the Louis XVI style, has elaborately-detailed carving, and unusual front with set-back side sections, six paw feet, and with shelved and mirrored interior. The underside has raised mark "Depose N. 25". Excellent condition, very rare to find. French, circa 1880. $300/600

9. French Bisque Poupée "Psyche" with Original Presentation Box and Mirror

11" (28 cm.) doll. 13" x 9" box. 7" mirror. A heavy card stock box with lavish padded

#9 mirror detail

#10

rose silk faille covering and ivory rope trim, hinges open to padded pale blue silk interior, that contains a bisque poupée and her costumes and mirror. The swivel head lady doll has blue enamel eyes, painted features, closed mouth with accented lips, pierced ears, blonde mohair wig over cork pate, shapely kid poupée body with gusset-jointing at hips, stitched and separated fingers and is wearing her original muslin chemise and earrings. Included is an original Psyche mirror with hinged sides allowing the mirror to tilt back and forth; the silvered-frame oval mirror has a reverse repousse design of winged Cupid and maker's stamp, and there are two additional costumes, undergarments, bonnet. The poupée is marked 2/0. Excellent condition, very sturdy body and lovely bisque. French, Gaultier, circa 1880, for the luxury trade. $1800/2800

10. 19th Century French Miniature Teal Blue Glassware

2" (5 cm.) In a rich teal blue color, the service includes a cake or cheese dish with domed lid and four matching glass cups with amber glass handles and hand-painted white enameled flower and berry designs. Included is a pale blue ribbed candle holder. The service is of superb luxury quality, likely sold in Giroux & Cie or similar Parisian luxury store of the mid-19th century. Excellent condition. Circa 1865, appropriately-sized for display with dolls about 22"-25". $300/500

11. French Automaton "Little Girl with Doll and Hair-Brush" by Leopold Lambert

19" (48 cm.) Standing upon a velvet covered base is a bisque-head doll with amber brown glass paperweight eyes, dark eyeliner, richly-painted lashes and brows, accented nostrils, closed mouth with outlined lips, pierced ears, blonde mohair wig over cork pate, French carton torso and legs, wire upper arms, bisque forearms. She is wearing her original magenta silk costume fashioned in the workshops of Lambert overseen by Eugenie Lambert, and holds a little all-bisque doll in her right hand and a hair-brush in the left, as though about to comb her doll's hair. When wound, the presentation is heightened by the movement, as the girl alternately lifts the doll, then the brush, while nodding and turning her head as though inspecting her workmanship; music play. Condition: generally excellent, some fraility to original costume, mechanism and music function well. Marks: Depose Tete Jumeau Bte SGDG 4 (doll) (original paper label indicating tune "Les cloches de Corneville" on underside). A very beautiful and original French automaton with enchanting movements of special interest in a doll milieu. French, Leopold Lambert, circa 1890. $5000/8000

12. Rare 19th Century Miniature Accessories for Doll's Table

4" (10 cm.) l. silver tray. Included is a fine silver dessert tray with filigree frame and handles, serving knife with mother-of-pearl handle and silver hallmarks, mother-of-pearl footed basket with gilt metal frame, porcelain three-footed bowl signed Limoges with early faux-fruit, and a very rare 2" velvet box whose fitted interior displays a three-piece silver place setting. Excellent condition. Mid/late-19th century. Appropriately sized for display with 16"-18" poupée. $300/600

13. Fine French Crystal Service

7" (18 cm.) h. decanter with stopper. Of fine crystal, including round tray with gilt edging, decanter with teardrop design and stopper, and six stemware glasses of very fine delicate quality. Excellent condition. Circa 1875. $300/400

14. French Salon Chair for Poupée with Silk Tufted Seat

11" (28 cm.) The elegantly-carved wooden side chair has original ebony finish with gilt stenciled designs, and its original tufted magenta silk seat with tiny silk-covered buttons. Excellent condition. French, circa 1870. $300/500

15. Wonderful French Bisque Poupée by Jumeau in Original Royal Historical Silk Costume

14" (36 cm.) Bisque swivel head on kid-edged bisque shoulder plate, very large blue glass paperweight inset eyes, dark eyeliner, painted lashes and brows, rose-blushed eye shadow, accented nostrils, closed mouth, pierced ears, blonde mohair wig over cork pate, French shapely kid poupée body, stitched and separated fingers. Condition: generally excellent, body very sturdy and clean except some finger wear. Marks: (artist marks on head) Jumeau Medaille d'Or Paris (body stamp). Comments: Emile Jumeau, circa 1880, the doll is wearing her original elaborate padded-silk gown in magenta and ivory colors, trimmed with gilt metallic threads and faux-jewels, likely representing royalty of European or Russian lineage. Value Points: exceptionally beautiful poupée with dramatic eyes and superb original costume, with original wooden stand. $3000/5000

16. Extremely Rare and Wonderful 19th Century Chinese Tea Shop with Rare Contents

26" (66 cm.) w. x 16"h. x 15"d. The wooden-framed shop has unusual arched front entry supported by richly laquered green and gold columns and two narrow side-front walls with display windows framed in cast brass; the facade has red lacquered finish and "Asiatica Tee Handlung" lettered sign and the brass-framed windows are set in blue painted walls with gold accents and applique images of Asian people. The lacquered finish continues around the sides and back with paper-framed engravings as accents. The floor is lithographed paper with heavy lacquered finish, and the side and back walls are completely fitted with shelving, slant bins and 16 tea drawers or cabinets, all with original red or black lacquered finish. There is a matching free standing counter of red lacquer with green lacquer top and brass coin slot, and a matching cast iron scale with brass trays. The shelves are lavishly fitted with an array of silk and paper-wrapped treasures, a carved bone frame, celluloid rickshaw, and, notably, 26 very rare tea tins with various lithographed scenes. A bisque doll with amber-complexion and original costume stands behind the counter. Excellent condition. Maker unknown, late-19th century shop of outstanding quality and complexity, rare contents. $5500/8500

17. French Porcelain Doll-Size Dinner Service
6" (15 cm.) footed tureen. Of fine white porcelain with glazed finish, blue borders and gilt pencil-stripe trim, and decorated with acorn finials and oak leaf designs, the service includes 5" and 6" lidded footed tureens, two 4" footed compotes, two footed sauce dishes with attached bases and lids (one with ladle), one open-top sauce dish, three graduated size platters, ten 5" plates, six 5" shallow bowls, four 6" plates, and four footed serving plates. Excellent condition. French, circa 1885. $400/600

18. Luxury Set of Doll's Cutlery in Original Box
5" (13 cm.) l. knife. 12' x 11" box. A wooden box with textured blue paper cover and padded ivory silk lining contains a complete set of doll-sized cutlery, including six knives, six forks, six spoons, six napkins rings, and six knife rests. Excellent unplayed with condition. For the luxury trade, early-20th century. $300/500

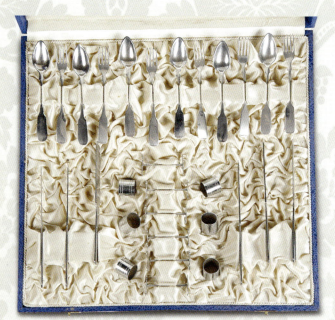

19. French All-Bisque Mignonette in Original Costume
5 ½" (14 cm.) Bisque swivel head on bisque torso, dark glass inset eyes, painted features, closed mouth, light brown mohair wig, pin-jointed bisque arms and legs, painted white stockings with magenta rims, black four-lace painted ankle boots, original blue silk dress with lace trim. Condition: tiny cheek rub. Marks: 2/0. Comments: French, circa 1885. Value Points: endearing facial expression, all-original body with shapely legs and rare style of painted boots for this model. $400/500

20. French Well-Laid Dining Table for Petite French Poupée
12" (30 cm.) x 8"table. 7"h. table. 10" chairs. The early dining table with spindle-carved legs is set for a feast for six, each setting with pewter underplate and porcelain shallow bowl, napkin ring and napkin, cutlery, and with 11 matching porcelain serving dishes, silver soft metal cruet set with glass bottles, wine service of fine crystal with round tray, decanter with stopper and six stemware glasses, and with a silver tinware table dust pan and brush, and, finally, a miniature red wine bottle from Chateau Moncontour. Also included are a pair of balloon-back chairs with red velvet upholstered seats and carved legs. Excellent condition. French, circa 1875. Appropriately sized for poupées 14"-16". $800/1200

21. Beautiful 19th Century Crystal Hanging Chandelier
6" (15 cm.) Suspending from a brass ceiling cover is an elaborate crystal chandelier with thin wire frame, alternating bands of small glass beads and larger prismatic beads, with cascading garlands of small beads, and prismatic tear drops dangling from the lower garland. Excellent condition. French, mid-19th century. $500/900

22. Petite French Bisque Poupée by Doleac in Original Silk Costume
14" (36 cm.) Bisque swivel head on bisque shoulder plate, blue enamel glass inset eyes with pronounced black pupils, painted features, closed mouth with center accent line, pierced ears, blonde mohair wig over cork pate, French kid poupée body with gusset-jointing at hips, knees, and elbows, stitched and separated fingers. Condition: generally excellent, tiny flake at front crown rim with original firing or hairline (under wig), body very sturdy. Marks: L. Depose 1 D. Comments: Louis Doleac, circa 1875. Value Points: the rare signed poupée with distinctive regal facial modeling of the Doleac poupée, is wearing her original ivory silk ensemble, undergarments, leather boots marked "1". $1800/2500

#25

the beautiful doll with gorgeous eyes wears her lovely factory-original costume. $300/500

24. Vintage Miniature Christmas Tree and Ornaments
11" (28 cm.) The miniature holiday tree has original wooden base and snow speckled branches and is decorated with miniature glass holiday balls and candles. Included are an assortment of additional miniature vintage glass balls. Excellent condition. Germany, early-20th century. $300/500

25. Tiny German Brown-Complexioned Bisque Doll with Original Costume
4" (10 cm.) Bisque socket head with brown complexion, brown glass inset eyes, painted features, closed mouth, black fleecy hair, brown composition five-piece body, wearing original red sateen dress with black lace trim, undergarments. Condition: generally excellent. Marks: 4/0. Comments: Germany, circa 1900. Value

23. Pretty Sonneberg Bisque Doll with Original Costume
13" (33 cm.) Bisque shoulder head with very plump lower cheeks, blue glass inset eyes with rich spiral threading, dark eyeliner, painted lashes, brush-stroked brows, accented eye corners, slightly-parted lips, four porcelain teeth, pierced ears, blonde mohair wig, kid gusset-jointed body with bisque forearms. Condition: old faint 1" hairline from left forehead rim (under wig), body especially clean and sturdy. Marks: 50/3. Comments: Sonneberg, circa 1880, designed to appeal to the French market. Value Points:

Points: rare to find in this tiny size, closed mouth, beautiful complexion. $300/400

26. Fine Early Miniature Rocking Horse

6" (15 cm.) The carved wooden horse in racing pose has original dappled brown hide finish, amber glass eyes, original leather harness and saddle, horsehair tail, and is posed on a metal rocking horse frame. Excellent condition. Germany, circa 1890, of very fine luxury quality and wonderfully-preserved. $600/900

27. Rare French Depose Automaton "Little Seated Girl with Her Dolls" by Leopold Lambert

13" (33 cm.) x 14" base. 14"h. A large wooden base with tapestry cover to lend the impression of carpeting, displays a seated bisque girl with blue glass eyes, original mohair lashes, painted features, open mouth, four porcelain teeth, pierced ears, brunette human hair wig, carton torso, hinged carton legs, bisque forearms, original silk and lace dress, undergarments, kid shoes, woven bonnet. She is holding a bisque doll in one hand, and a riding crop in her other hand. Nearby stands a paper mache toy donkey upon which is seated another bisque doll. When wound, a number of motions and activities take place in perfectly synchronized manner: the doll turns her head, nods, and blinks her eyes, alternately lifting the doll in her right hand in admiration, and then tapping the donkey with the riding crop; meanwhile her feet kick up and down in delight, and music plays. Condition: generally excellent, music and mechanism function well. Marks: SH 1039 7 dep (head) L.B. (key) (original paper tune label). Comments: Leopold Lambert, the automaton model was deposed in 1894 and in his patent notes Lambert said, "I took careful note of the movements made by the child and I have managed to imitate the entire range of these movements". Value Points: rare and delightful automaton with wonderful and realistic movements. $6000/9000

- 15 -

28. Very Rare German Wooden Shoe Store with Hanging Sign and Original Filled Shoe Boxes

28" (71 cm.) A large one-room wooden store with originally-painted yellow front columns with black accents, and green painted exterior walls, has an elaborately-constructed interior with built-in shelves on back and one side wall, a side staircase with railing, and a balcony with railing. Original wall paper peeks behind the shelving, and the original floor paper is a parquet design. An unusually-shaped oval free-standing counter, two wooden chairs with green velvet upholstery, and two shoe-fitting stools with slant tops furnish the store. The counter and shelving are painted to match the frame with faux-marble painted medallions. The store in ready for business with 55 boxes of shoes (actually containing shoes), most with metallic shoe designs on the boxes, along with 18 empty shoe boxes, and 6 pairs of unboxed shoes. The center niche displays belts, more hanging shoes, and socks in their original boxes. There are enamel shoe signs along the staircase, and a very rare cast iron hanging sign with a shoe symbol hangs at the side of the store. Excellent condition, a very rare and wonderfully-filled store, with unusual architectural features such as oval counter and hanging sign. $4500/7500

29. Rare German Wooden Caravan by Gottschalk
19" (48 cm.) l. x 7 ½" w. x 8" h. The wooden caravan with metal spoked wheels has original cream painted finish with blue stencil trim and green painted shutters, porch with side railings, pillars and detachable steps. The side walls hinge open for access to the two-room interior with center door and two windows, and having original wall and floor papers, some various contents. Excellent condition. Moritz Gottschalk, circa 1910, the rare model was presented in the company's annual catalog offerings, and is quite rare to find. $1200/1800

30. Tiny German Wooden Flower Shop and Various Potted Flowers, Attributed to Gottschalk
9" (23 cm.) k. x 4"d. x 5"h. The open-front wooden shop has original blue painted finish with stencil trim, original papered interior, and contains a three-stepped shelved arrangement that is filled with various potted flowers; an exterior trellis and window box are also filled, and also included are 5 additional shelves and racks of flowers. There are more than 50 potted flowers overall. Excellent condition. Germany, attributed to Gottschalk, circa 1910. $700/1200

31. Wonderful German Wooden Dollhouse Rooms with Original Furnishings
33" (84 cm.) l. x 14" h. x 15"d. The wooden doll house has two rooms with opening door between that has an etched glass window, each room with a three-part window against the back wall and having original valance. The house has fancy columns at the front and original cream painted finish with gold accents. The wall and floor papers are original and a chandelier hangs in each room. The wooden furnishings, with original cream finish trimmed in gilt including a curio cabinet, desk with mirror, settee and two

#31 detail

chairs, marble top table, two pedestals, and easel are by Paul Leonard, and there are additional other furnishings including grand piano and baby cradle. Of special note are two small bisque dolls in pink velvet costumes seated on a bear rug, that were featured in the oil painting displayed on the easel. Accessories include ormolu-framed prints, and other wall hangings, attached tin fireplace, tin Maerklin parlor stove with profile of woman's head, Christmas tree, white bisque busts, ormolu tiered dessert plate, oil lamps, and an arrangement of frame, busts and figurines atop the grand piano. There is a bisque dollhouse lady and gentleman, he with rarer sculpted moustache. Excellent condition. Germany, Paul Leonard, circa 1900, a wonderful house with many accessories and activities. $3500/4500

32. Petite German Wooden Pewter Shop with Rare Goods, Attributed to August Hermann
22" (56 cm.) l. x 10"d. x 13"h. The wooden-frame store with two angled side walls and two store front display windows has elaborately-carved facade, original dark wood finish, original lithographed wall and floor papers, and a shelved arrangement on the back wall with a centering display niche. There is a matching counter and hanging shelf. A silver-metal candleabra suspends, and the shop is filled with more than 50 miniature pewter and silver metal accessories and serving pieces, several in original boxes. A bisque gentleman with distinguished grey hair and beard stands in attendance. Excellent condition. Germany, circa 1890, attributed to August Hermann, tghe store is marked on the underside "17 4/0 1/10 T/b". $1800/3200

33. Rare French Pewter Tea Service by C.B.G. in Original Labeled Gift Box
2 ½" (6 cm.) A round heavy card box box with decorative paper covers and gilt edging has original straw filling in which is nestled a pewter tea service comprising footed tea pot with lid, footed sugar with double handles and lid, creamer, four cups and saucers, and four spoons. Each of the handles is richly detailed and the lids are topped with tiny bead finials. The inside of the lid has original paper label

- 20 -

with gilt stenciling "The Metal Anglais, Solidite Salubrite, Depose C.B.G." indicating that the service was deposed and was of finest quality. Cuperly, Blondel and Gerbeau, France, the CBG symbol was registered in 1873 and appeared on their finest works. Excellent condition, some repair to box. $300/500

34. French Silver Metal Tea Service for Doll in Original Presentation Box

3" (8 cm.) h. tea pot. 15" x 10" box. A light-wood box with blue paper cover and gold stenciled lettering "The Service" (Tea Service) hinges open to a velvet lined interior with original arrangement of silver metal tea service for six of great luxury, each piece with richly-embossed detail. The service includes lidded teapot, lidded sugar, creamer, six cups, six saucers, six dessert plates, six spoons, six napkins, and a gold-plated sugar tong. The box bears the maker's initials S.G. with shield mark. Excellent unplayed with condition. French, circa 1890. $500/800

35. Early Wooden Carriage with Luggage and Driver

26" (66 cm.) overall. 15" carriage only. 7" man. A wooden carriage with original red and black paint and gold stencil trim, has wooden spoked wheels, wooden attachments at the front for horse, lanterns, hinged side passenger door, driver's seat, and various baggage. A bisque head dollhouse man with brown painted hair and sideburns, and wearing unusual and original leather coat serves as the driver. Very good condition. Circa 1880, probably Germany. $800/1200

38. French "Nouveaute de Paris" Toiletries for Poupée or Small Bébé

9" (23 cm.) x 5". A heavy stock card with stenciled label "Nouveaute de Paris" and "Depose C.L. France" has an arrangement of tiny accessories and toiletries for larger poupée or small bébé, comprising "Petunia d'Amerique" perfume bottle, wrapped soaps, opera glass, hair pins, powder puff, mirror, and jewelry. Excellent condition. Late-19th Century. $300/500

39. Beautiful French Bisque Poupée Attributed to Jumeau

15" (38 cm.) Bisque swivel head on kid-edged bisque shoulder plate, pale blue glass enamel inset eyes with darker outer rims, dark eyeliner, painted lashes, feathered brows, accented nostrils, closed mouth, pierced ears, blonde mohair wig over cork pate, French kid gusset-jointed body, wearing lovely antique costume comprising blue silk skirt, black velvet fitted jacket, black velvet bonnet, undergarments, leather ankle boots, earrings. Condition: generally excellent, body somewhat worn and quill pen lettering of unknown significance on the torso. Marks: 2. Comments: Jumeau, circa 1875. Value Points: very beautiful eyes enhanced by dramatic eye decoration. $2000/3000

36. French Cast Metal Gilt Vitrine with Depose Mark

9" (23 cm.) The heavy cast metal vitrine in the Louis XVI style has cabriole legs with curved feet, elaborately scrolled door frame, mirrored back, hinged back door, and is marked with raised letters "Depose N. 23" on the underside. Along with two plants in wooden pots. Excellent condition. French, circa 1875. $300/500

37. Pair, German All-Bisque Bride and Groom in Antique Wedding Costumes

4" (10 cm.) Each is all-bisque with swivel head and peg-jointed limbs, cobalt blue glass eyes, painted features, closed mouth, auburn or blonde mohair wig, painted shoes and socks. Condition: generally excellent. Marks: 1. Comments: Germany, circa 1890. Value Points: the little couple wear their factory original costumes of the wedding couple. $400/600

40. Rare French Bisque Poupée with Sculpted Hair as Gentleman attributed to Barrois

14" (36 cm.) Solid domed bisque shoulder head with sculpted short brown hair with detailed comb marks and forehead curls, painted blue down-glancing eyes with thick upper eyeliner and painted lashes and brows, accented nostrils, closed mouth with accent line between the lips, kid poupée body with slender shaping, stitched and separated fingers, wearing antique gentleman's costume (some moth holes) with wonderful embroidered silk vest. Condition: generally excellent. Marks: 3. Comments: attributed to Barrois, circa 1870, a nearly identical model is shown in *The Encyclopedia of French Dolls* by Theimer, page 50. Value Points: rare to find poupée with especially fine detail of hair sculpting. $2000/3000

41. French Musical Doll's Piano of Napoleon III Epoch, Rare Accessories
11" (28 cm.) h. x 12"w. The ebonized wooden upright piano has faux keyboard with carved detail, and is edged with bronze gilt borders, emblems (one of lyre), candle holders, and side handles. The lid hinges open revealing the piano's original purpose as luxury candy container, and later use as necessaire. Hidden inside the piano is a keywind music box that begins to play when wound and the lid lifted. Included with the piano is a pair of gilded metal three-arm candelabra and a rare French two-piece epergne with hand-painted designs. Excellent condition. French, mid-19th century, Napoleon III epoch, the piano is very rare. $1200/1600

42. French Salon Dog with Amber Glass Eyes
7" (18 cm.) The firm-shaped dog is lavishly covered with white fur except for shaved face and legs, has carved open mouth, amber glass eyes, upright ears. Very good condition. French, circa 1880. $300/500

43. Wonderful French Bisque Poupée by Duval-Denis with Trousseau and Rare Inventory

17" (43 cm.) Pink-tinted porcelain shoulder head with plump facial shape, rich cobalt blue glass enamel inset eyes, delicately-painted lashes and brows, accented nostrils, closed mouth with accented center line, unpierced ears, brunette hand-tied human hair wig over cork pate, kid

poupée body with gusset-jointing at hips and knees, porcelain arms to above the elbows. Condition: generally excellent. Marks: Brevete D.D. SGDG (stamp on torso) Au Pere Noel (shop label). Comments: Duval-Denis, successor to the Blampoix firm for a two-year period only, 1861-1863; signed D.D. poupées are from this short period only, and this example was sold in the Paris toy shop, Au Pere Noel. Value Points: very rare-to-find poupée with gorgeous face and complexion, beautiful porcelain arms, along with her original trunk, trousseau and extremely rare hand-written inventory of the clothes that she owns titled "Liste de Trousseau de ma poupée". The poupée wears an exceptional gown of ivory and peach silk taffeta with matching bonnet, and owns four additional gowns (one very frail), black taffeta jacket, brushed velvet and woolen coat, plaid cape, fur collar, three fine bonnets and one wooden hat box, bridal coronne, two chemisettes, three pairs of sleevelets, two night caps, rose satin stays, various shifts and undergarments, opera glasses, shoes, parasol, and a few assorted other accessories. The trousseau and inventory have been preserved in an early French doll trunk. (The doll and trousseau were featured in an article in *Antique Doll Collector*, June 2009). $6000/9000

was designed as miniature versions of the life-size furniture that was the specialty of Maison Huret, with the purpose of display with the signature Huret poupée; luxury objects at the time, the furnishings are very rare to find today. $2000/3000

45. Collection of Miniature Frames and Engravings
2" (5 cm.) Each of gilt metal with easel back, the collection includes a trilogy frame with chromolithographs of three young girls, a double frame with lithographs of young ladies, matched ornate easel frames with lithographs of Kaiser Wilhelm I and his wife Augusta, and five additional frames. Excellent condition. Circa 1890. $300/500

44. French Salon Table and Chair for Poupée from Maison Huret
12" (30 cm.) Each is of metal with spiral-twist design of the frame and original gilt finish and original crushed velvet upholstery, including arm chair with green stamp "Maison Huret Boulevard Montmartre 22 Paris" on the underside; and pedestal table with brass nail edging above original wool fringe, and having original paper label "Maison Boul Montmartre 22" on underside sateen cover. Structurally excellent, finish is original albeit rubbed. French, Maison Huret, the furniture

46. French Porcelain Miniature Tête-à-Tête Tea Service

9" (23 cm.) l. tray. Of finest white porcelain, decorated with gold leaf borders and hand-painted floral, ribbon and garland designs, including scroll-shaped tray, lidded teapot, oval sugar bowl, creamer, and two cups and saucers. The service is marked is S in shield design. Excellent condition. $300/600

47. French Bronze Salon Table with Ram Head Motif, With Pair of Urns

A luxury quality bronze table with rich gold leaf finish has shaped white marble top, and table frame enhanced with acanthus border, horned ram heads at each corner, and cabriole-style legs terminating in hooves. French, circa 1865, of fine luxury quality, possible for Giroux & Cie. Included is a pair of antique Chinese porcelain urns with original lids. Excellent condition. $900/1300

48. Superb French Miniature Tea Service by Lebeu, Milliet & Cie

8" (20 cm.) diam. tray. A fine quality creamy faience tea service decorated with a delicate Chinoiserie pattern in shades of pale green, rose and blue, with delicately painted flowers and buds in exquisite detail, including large round tray, lidded teapot, lidded sugar, creamer, and four cups and saucers. Each piece is marked L.M. & Cie with green stamp. Excellent condition. French, mid-19th century, Lebeuf Milliet & Cie, the product of the French firm is highly celebrated and few pieces are known of their miniature work. $500/800

49. German Bisque Miniature Child, 192, by Kammer and Reinhardt

6" (15 cm.) Bisque socket head, brown glass sleep eyes, painted features, open mouth, four porcelain teeth, blonde mohair wig, five-piece composition body, beautiful antique dress and bonnet, undergarments, painted shoes and socks. Marks: 192 3/0. Condition: generally excellent. Comments: Kammer and Reinhardt, circa 1910. Value Points: very sweet all-original miniature doll. $300/400

51. Collection of Doll's Desk Accessories and Journals

4 ½" (11 cm.) globe. Appropriately-sized for display with poupées about 16"-20", including world globe with carved wooden base and revolving globe, 4" red leatherette Papeterie with tiny envelopes and stationary; brown leather case, and ten various miniature journals dating from tiny 1 ¼"h. "Bijou Almanack 1859" to 1905 to 1938. Very good condition. $500/800

49.1. French Woven Doll Furnishings

20" (51 cm.) l. chaise lounge. Each is woven wicker furniture for garden or sun room, perfect for display with bebes about 20"-24". Including chaise lounge and settee, each with original tufted chintz upholstery; the pieces are complementary although not originally matching. Excellent condition. French, circa 1890. $500/700

50. Set of French Miniature Books in Original Cabinet

6" (15 cm.) cabinet. 1 ¾" books. A wooden cabinet with bombe-shaped sides and beveled glass door is covered with silk brocade fabric and contains within seven miniature French books ranging from "Quelques Fables" to "Aladdin", dated 1896. Very good condition, set incomplete and books are well-read. French, circa 1896, rare to find. $300/500

52. 19th Century Doll's Leather Desk Accessories and Pewter Inkwell

6" (15 cm.) l. pad. A brown leather desk pad with gold-tooled embossing unfolds to reveal the four-cornered pad and hidden folio compartment, along with matching blotter, and with matching card folder. Included is 2 ¾" pewter inkwell with candleholder and powder. For display with 20"-22" poupées. Excellent condition. French, circa 1890. $400/600

#54 detail shown actual size

53. French Bisque Poupée by Barrois in Gentleman's Costume

15" (38 cm.) Bisque swivel head with flat-cut neck socket on kid-edged bisque shoulder-plate, pale complexion with rosy cheeks, brilliant cobalt blue glass enamel eyes, dark eyeliner, feathered lashes and brows, closed mouth with accented lips, un-pierced ears, fleecy wig, kid poupée body with gusset-jointing at elbows, hips and knees, stitched and separated fingers, wearing antique woolen gentleman's suit with vest, tie, key chain, leather shoes. Condition: generally excellent, body especially sturdy. Marks: E. 3 Depose B. Comments: Barrois, circa 1860. Value Points: rare neck swivel system, brilliant eyes, well-preserved original body on the early poupée. $2000/2800

54. Collection of Miniature Shakespeare Books and Revolving Bookcase

9" (23 cm.) bookcase, 6" revolving bookcase. 2" books. The three-shelved wooden wall book case holds a complete set of 40 miniature works (each 2"h) by Shakespeare published by Allied Newspapers in 1932, each book with an illustrated frontispiece of a play scene, with marbled end-papers and black leatherette cloth covers with lightly-printed titled; the bookcase was originally sold with the set of books. Excellent condition of bookcase and books. Along with a revolving wooden bookcase containing other miniature Shakespeare works, published by David Bryce and Co of Glasgow, early-20th century. Bookcase excellent, books are quite worn. And with a decorative bonze statue of pheasant, excellent condition. $800/1200

55. Outstanding German "Les Modes Parisienne" Milliner's Shop by Christian Hacker

32" (81 cm.) w. x 17"h. (38" including legs) x 19"d. The wooden-framed shop is designed to display from both front and back, allowing a vision of the shop from display windows, as well as easy access to the store interior for child's play. The entire interior and exterior shop has original painted finish of wood-grained ochre with brown trim and stenciling; the floor is painted marbleized-green. The exterior back wall has two large display windows with interior wide shelving and lights, centered by an opening door with upper window. Above the door is an original banner sign with well-detailed lithographed, symbolic designs including crests of various countries, a seated lady, a lion, village and sea scenes, the intertwined initials E.L. and the name "Les Modes Parisienne, 20 rue Bergere". The interior back walls are designed with visual access to the street displays, and the side walls are fitted with eight drawers and a center display niche on each side; the drawers have blue and gold lithographed paper covers. There is a hanging light, two pulley-fixtures that allow canvas window shades to be drawn when the shop is closed, a free standing matching counter with beautiful paint work, and two hidden drawers. The shop is lavishly filled with bolts of fabric, trims, accessories, some garments on display, bonnets, hat boxes, decorative boxes, buttons, sample book of silks, and little books of lace samples. Excellent condition, door window glass cracked, original finish well-preserved throughout. German, Christian Hacker, circa 1875 for the French market. $5500/7500

Close up of store label

"Les Modes Parisienne" at 20 rue Bergere in Paris was one of the more prominent Parisian fashion journals of the mid-19th century; it is unknown if this miniature shop was commissioned uniquely as a promotional object for "Les Modes Parisienne" journal, or whether it was a stock piece that took advantage of the journal's name and popularity. What is certain is the luxury quality and details of the miniature shop.

niche of her original cardboard box, with three other compartments containing a blue and white checkered dress with lace Bertha collar along with undergarments and woven bonnet, various tiny threads, scissors, buttons, and four rolled cotton fabric pieces designed for the child to use sewing more costumes for her doll. Marks: German 390 A 10/0 M. Circa 1900, the presentation box is original and complete. $800/1200

58. German All-Bisque Miniature Doll and Costumes in Candy Box Trunk

4" (10 cm.) x 2" trunk. 3 ½" doll. An all-bisque doll with painted features, closed mouth, brunette mohair wig, pin-jointed bisque arms and legs, painted socks and brown one-strap shoes, lace dress is presented in a paper-lace edged candy trunk with silk lining, an additional costume and accessories. Excellent condition of doll, box is worn. Germany, for the French market, circa 1900. $200/400

56. German Bisque Dollhouse Lady with Trousseau

14" (36 cm.) x 9" box. 7" doll. A heavy stock box with white paper covers and gold edging has a fitted interior displaying a bisque dollhouse lady with sculpted short brown curly hair, painted facial features, muslin body, bisque lower limbs, painted white stockings and black shoes, wearing hand-made white cotton undergarments, along with two additional jackets, two skirts, blouse, three bonnets, and various toiletry articles. Excellent condition, some little holes and repairs in plaid skirt. Marks: 317. Circa 1890. $600/900

59. Petite German Bisque Character, 114, "Gretchen" by Kammer and Reinhardt

7" (18 cm.) Bisque socket head, painted facial features, closed mouth with downcast pouting expression, one-stroke brows, blonde mohair wig with side-coiled braids, composition and wooden

57. German Bisque Miniature Doll in Original Sewing Presentation Box

9 ½" (24 cm.) x 10" box. 6" doll. A bisque-head doll with blue glass eyes, painted features, closed mouth, brunette mohair wig, five-piece composition body with painted shoes and socks, is arranged in a center

ball-jointed body, wonderful antique costume. Condition: generally excellent. Marks: K*R 114 19. Comments: Kammer and Reinhardt, circa 1910, the model "Gretchen" from their art character series. Value Points: beautiful bisque and painting, original body and body finish, original wig and costume. $700/1000

60. Petite German Wooden Milliner's Shop

15" (38 cm.) "l. x 7"h. x 6"d. The small wooden shop with open front has arched pediment back and ribbed

front columns, built-in shelving at back walls, original wall and floor papers, and original wooden store counter. The store is fitted with an assortment of bolts of vintage fabric, ribbons, laces and trim, and a bisque doll with sculpted blonde hair stands behind the counter. Excellent condition. Germany, circa 1900, rare charming petite size in original state of preservation. $700/1100

61. Set of Celluloid Doll Accessories in Original Box

3 ½" (9 cm.) diam. box. A round card stock box with decorative gilt papers is silk lined and contains a variety of accessories for small bébé including hand mirror, brush, powder puff, lidded jar. Very good condition. Circa 1900. $200/300

62. Miniature Doll Accessories in Original Box

4" (10 cm.) A heavy card stock box opens to reveal a fitted interior with a variety of accessories for bébés about 20"-22", including three decorative combs, one long comb (3 teeth missing), powder puff, jar, and hand mirror. Very good condition, some box wear. Circa 1920. $100/300

#61   #62

- 33 -

63. German Handwind Mechanical Musical Vignette "The Music Lession" by Zinner and Sohne

13" (33 cm.) x 9 ½" base. 6" dolls. Four bisque miniature dolls with glass eyes, open mouth, four teeth, blonde mohair wigs, antique costumes, are posed upon a wooden platform with lithographed-paper cover. A wooden music stand at the center holds sheet music, one girl holds a sheet, and three girls hold musical instruments. When wound, music plays, they turn their heads side to side, and move their arms as though playing the instruments they hold. Very good condition, some fading and dustiness of papers and costumes, mechanism and music function well. Germany, Zinner and Sohne, circa 1890, a luxury presentation by that firm with four little dolls. $2000/3000

64. Outstanding German Wooden Toy Store Well-Laden for the Holidays

28" (71 cm.) l. x 19"h. x 14"d. A large wooden store front with hinged front display window that can open for easy play has built in ceiling-height shelving with arched crest at the back and low shelving that extends around the sides. There is an unusual scalloped display niche at the center back, a built-in faux-clock, and beaded detail of trim around the front and at the bottom of the decorative wall border. The border is a wonderful original lithograph depicting children at play. There is a matching free-standing counter, tin cash register, and hanging wooden chandelier. An early miniature Christmas tree stands at one corner. The shop is filled with dozens of miniature dolls and toys including wooden Erzebirge vehicles and action piece such as Ferris wheels, bisque and all-bisque dolls (some in original boxes), miniature blocks in original box, pull-toy paper mache horses on original wooden bases, ship, early tin bi-planes, and a superb early wooden Polichinelle theatre with lever movement. The store has original wall and floor papers, and original exterior paint. A porcelain lady doll stands in attendance. Very good/excellent condition, wood separation on one side wall. Germany, the store attributed to Albin Schonherr, circa 1900. $3500/5500

65. Outstanding German Wooden Kitchen Cabinet for Child's Play

53" (135 cm.) h. x 24"w. x 15"d. Designed to fit against a wall, the flat-backed cabinet shelf of pinewood with wood-grained oak finish enhanced with brown stencils has various hanging hooks and shelves, dark green faux-slate counter, and lower cabinet with double doors. The cabinet is filled to overflowing with child-sized kitchenware and dishes, centered by a large tin stove with claw feet (probably Maerklin). Surrounding the stove are a myriad of kitchen utensils including painted-tin coffee grinder with copper lid, painted tin scales with two brass pans, wooden-based slicer, tin laundry tub with enamel blue scenes of windmill and village along with various pieces of ironed laundry and laundry accessories, cookie cutters, another scale, other sundry ware, and a rare lithographed-tin "grocery list" sign ("Merktafel") with movable buttons to designate needed supplies. The cabinet is decorated with a plethora of blue and white porcelain dishes and kitchen tools including: rare stacking carry-out lunch plates in original wire frame, large lidded tureen, three porcelain bowls with bent-wire frames, rare spoon holder with wooden pedestal and porcelain cap, having six soft-metal spoons, six wooden-handled utensils with blue-decorated porcelain parts including pie-crimper, sieves, ladle and rolling pin, six brass knives with blue-decorated porcelain handles signed "Uchatius Bronce", coffee pot with matching sugar and creamer, three other creamers, six cups and saucers, nine various dinner plates or bowls, six small bowls, two gravy boats, wall boxes for "Salz" and "Mehl", oil cruet, funnel and a porcelain faux-clock. Excellent condition, three cups with repair, few other minor flakes. Germany, circa 1910, an outstanding and extremely rare child's play cabinet with rare accessories. $3000/5000

65.1. German Bisque Child, 119, by Handwerck

28" (71 cm.) Bisque socket head, blue glass sleep eyes, painted features, open mouth, four porcelain teeth, pierced ears, brunette mohair wig, composition and wooden ball-jointed body, wearing antique cotton dress and pinafore, undergarments, stockings, shoes. Condition: generally excellent, original body finish. Marks: 119-13 Handwerck 5 Germany. Comments: Handwerck, circa 1900. Value Points: pretty dolly-face model with fine quality of bisque, antique costume. $400/600

#65 detail

#65 detail

#65 detail

#65 detail

67. German All-Bisque Doll with Tiny Kitten

3 ½" (9 cm.) One-piece bisque head and torso, blue glass eyes, painted features, closed mouth, blonde mohair wig, peg-jointed bisque arms and legs, painted white socks and black one-strap shoes, antique checkered costume. Excellent condition. Germany, circa 1900, including a tiny vintage tabby kitten with green glass eyes. $200/300

#67

68. German Porcelain Rooster Tea Set and Basket of Glassware

4" (10 cm.) h. teapot. Of white porcelain, the teapot, sugar and creamer are figural designs of crowing rooster, along with three porcelain cups (set incomplete). Also included is a woven handled basket, 4" x 3", containing six footed glasses. Excellent condition, Circa 1910. $200/400

69. French Etrennes Presentation Box "The Little Baker"

8 ½" (22 cm.) x 6" box. 5" doll. A light-wooden box with decorative paper covers and a lithograph of little boy in baker's costume on the lid, hinges open to reveal a well-fitted interior, with all-bisque doll having painted features, blue eyes, closed mouth, blonde mohair wig, pin-jointed arms and legs, wearing chef's costume and cap, along with a collection of foods including chops, sausages, breads, rolls, and more, all still tied into the original presentation. Excellent unplayed with condition. For the French market, presented in the department store Etrennes catalogs, circa 1900. $500/800

70. German Wooden Cabinet with Metal Stove and Blue Enamelware

24" (61 cm.) The tall kitchen wooden cabinet with original creamy white paint and blue pencil stripe trim has two drawers, shelf, counter top and brass pot hanging rod. Arranged

66. German Wooden Two-Story Blue Roof Dollhouse by Moritz Gottschalk

20" (51 cm.) excluding chimney. The two-story wooden dollhouse has original lithographed paper cover on interior and exterior, with faux-brick facade, printed second-floor door with exterior balcony having metal grill that matches the grill on the front porch railing, The first floor front door, having classic Gottschalk silver knob, opens and closes, and there is carved detail on the gable roof that matches the carved roof line on the sides of the house. The entire front hinges open to reveal original wall and floor papers of the interior. Very good condition, original papers with some crinkling at the front. Mortiz Gottschalk, circa 1890. $1200/1800

#68

on the cabinet is a tinplate toy stove (probably Bing) with chrome oven door and original pots, and various kitchen tools. Accessories are arranged on the shelves and hooks, including a dark blue enamel coffee pot and six cups and plates, blue tin coffee grinder, ten blue tinplate molds, seven enamelware pots, five enamelware spoons and sieves, tin cookie cutters, and more. Excellent condition. Germany, circa 1890. $800/1200

71. German Wax Doll in Original Elaborate Folklore Costume

18" (46 cm.) Wax shoulder head with blue glass inset eyes, painted facial features, closed mouth with downcast lips, brunette mohair wig in long braid, muslin body with paper mache lower limbs, glued knit striped stockings, painted fancy black heeled ankle boots with red and white trim. Condition: good with some typical fading and craquelure on face. Comments: Germany, circa 1875. Value Points: all-original and unplayed with, having elaborate original folklore costume and cap, fancily-painted boots. $500/700

#69

74. German Bisque Miniature Doll with Toys

5" (13 cm.) Bisque socket head, blue glass sleep eyes, painted features, open mouth with teeth, blonde mohair wig, five-piece paper mache body, painted shoes, wearing original folklore costume of Brittany with embroidered detail, marked S&C 293, by Franz Schmidt. Included with the little boy are his two toys: a paper mache dog with jointed limbs, and a little bisque doll with chenille body on wooden sled. Excellent condition. Germany, circa 1910. $300/400

72. German Wooden Holiday Toy Stall with St. Nicholas

15" (38 cm.) l. x 12"h. x 6". d. The open-front wooden stall with shaped column sides and slant roof is filled to overbrimming with toys and accessories for Christmas, including wooden Erzebirge figures, toy soldiers, paper mache figures and animals, merry-go-round, toy houses, and more. Included is a paper mache St. Nicholas candy container who stands alongside the shop, another Santa on a sleigh, Christmas tree with red ball decorations and original wooden stand. Excellent condition, shop frame has some chips. Germany, early-20th century. $3500/5500

73. German Porcelain Lady as Toy Peddler with Tin Cart of Miniature Toys

7" (18 cm.) Porcelain shoulder head lady with sculpted hair and painted facial features, muslin body, porcelain limbs, wearing antique cotton costume and apron, stands beside her two-wheeled tin peddler cart with original creamy white finish decorated with blue striping. The toy cart is filled to overbrimming with miniature dolls and toys. Excellent condition. Germany, late-19th century, the cart may be Maerklin. A wonderful presentation with delightful little treasures. $1200/1600

75. Wonderful French Mechanical Carousel with Rare Animal Figures for Au Paradis des Enfants

20" (51 cm.) A fanciful carousel is richly decorated with mirrored center pedestal, red sateen covered base, colorful mercury glass balls, red and white striped awning decorated with gold metal fringe and gold ormolu border. Suspended from the outer edge of the awning are four bisque head children, each riding a carousel animal, two on classic ponies, another on a merry pink pig, and the fourth on a glass-eyed bunny. When wound, the carousel twirls about in a merry way, and music plays. Excellent condition, some staining on awning, costumes a bit dusty, mechanism and music function well. There is an original label on the base "Au Paradis des Enfants..." indicating the toy was presented by the luxury Parisian toy store. A rare and absolutely charming vignette with wonderful decorations and delightful music and motion. $3000/6000

76. French "Porcelaine Service" in Original Box with Sevres Blue Dishes

18" (46 cm.) x 12" 5"h. chocolate pot. A light wooden box with decorative paper covers has original paper label on the lid, "Porcelaine Service"; the box hinges open to a beautifully-fitted interior featuring superb white porcelain dishes with rich cobalt blue decorations for which the Sevres porcelain works were known. The porcelain pieces are richly shaped and the cobalt blue decorations are further enhanced with gold trim. The service includes lidded chocolate or coffee pot, lidded sugar, creamer, two sauce dishes, fruit bowl, small bowl, four cups and saucers, six plates, six spoons, and serving fork and knife, that are neatly arranged on the shelved base and interior lid. Excellent condition. French, circa 1890, a luxury and well-preserved service. $700/1000

77. French Porcelain "Rosebud" Tea Service

6" (15 cm.) h. tea pot. Of fine white porcelain with gold edging, blue bands, and decorated with dainty pink rosebuds and leaves, the service comprises lidded coffee pot, lidded sugar, creamer, fruit bowl, two dessert serving plates, four cups, four saucers, and four little plates. Excellent condition. French, circa 1885, the service would display beautifully with bébés about 22"-26". $300/500

78. Fine German Porcelain Miniature Tea Service with Karlsbad Labelling

Of fine white porcelain, with cobalt blue abstract decorations heightened with gold leaf, and with a center medallion label "Karlsbad" on each piece, the set comprises shaped tray, lidded teapot, lidded sugar, creamer, six cups and six saucers. Excellent condition, beautiful shape of pot and tray. Germany, circa 1880. $300/500

79. 19th Century Miniature Cordial Service in Original Wooden Box
9" (23 cm.) x 7" case. 4" decanter. A carved wooden cabinet hinges open to a paper lined interior with lift-out bottom tray containing a blown glass decanter with stopper and ten stemmed glasses, each with ribbed design. Excellent condition. Circa 1890, maker unknown. $200/400

80. German Miniature Silver and Pewter Cutlery
2" (5 cm.) cruet set. Including three cards or box with soft metal or pewter cutlery still attached, the blue box with fine pewter quality service for two with matching napkin rings and knife rests. And with a soft metal cruet set with amber glass bottles. Excellent condition. Germany, circa 1900, very rare to find on original cards. $200/400

81. Superb English Doll-Sized Burled Walnut Cabinet with Velvet-Edged Shelving
28" (71 cm.) h. x 22"w. x 8"d. The finely-shaped burled walnut cabinet has

#80

two arched doors with six-pane windows at the front and arched three-pane windows at each side. A bombe-shaped drawer is at the bottom and the feet are elaborately carved talons. There are cast hardware drawer pulls, and the shelving with elaborately shaped front edges has original velvet covering. Included is a porcelain doll-sized service comprising lidded tureen, 2 lidded casserole dishes, footed bowl, 4 footed serving dishes, 2 relish dishes, gravy boat with attached under plate, oval platter, round platter, and 15 assorted plates or shallow soup bowls. Excellent condition. Mid-19th century. $800/1200

pierced ears, blonde mohair wig over cork pate, French kid poupée body with shapely torso, padded detail of bosom, gusset-jointing of hips, knees and elbows, stitched and separated fingers, wearing original grey linen suit with black velvet and lace trim, undergarments, early hand-sewn leather slippers, lace-edged bonnet, white fur fox-tail muff. Condition: generally excellent. Comments: French, circa 1870. Value Points: exceptionally beautiful poupée in pristine unplayed with condition, body especially sturdy and clean, gorgeous eyes and complexion. $3500/4500

83. Fine Tiny French Porcelain Wash Set with Bronze Edging

3 ½" (9 cm.) x 2 ½" tray. A fine white porcelain tray is edged with a bronze fitted frame, and included is a wash bowl and pitcher, and four small accessories, each decorated with floral design. Several pieces are marked Limoges. Excellent condition. $300/500

84. French Porcelain Tiny Wash Set in Original Silk Lined Box

3 ½" (9 cm.) x 3 ½" box. 1 ½"h. pitcher. Inside a silk lined box with fitted niches is preserved a fine white porcelain wash set with bowl, pitcher, and three small bowls, each with gold and floral decoration, signed Limoges. Excellent condition. $200/400

85. Fine Early-19th Century French Music Salon with Le Maire Shop Label

14" (36 cm.) h. x 17"w. x 13"d. Designed with Grecian influence to appear as though a summer musical or theatre

82. Superb French Bisque Poupée with Gorgeous Face and Original Costume

22" (56 cm.) Bisque swivel head on kid-edged bisque shoulder plate, brilliant cobalt blue glass enamel eyes, dark eyeliner, painted lashes, feathered brows, mauve-blushed eye shadow, softly-blushed cheeks, closed mouth with accented lips, accented nostrils,

room, the wooden salon has exterior paper cover to simulate marble, with ribbed columns at the side front that are repeated on the interior, framing the arched side windows and forming an entrance at the proscenium steps at the rear of the room. The proscenium rises above an arched raised floor and there are display niches at each side. Original paper to suggest parquet covers the floor and gold leaf papers enhance each column support. The room is furnished with an early wooden harp that appears original, four chairs, two wooden columns with carved bone statues, violin, several carved bone objects including a sewing basket, music stand, and two early German porcelain dolls. The stamp of the early Parisian toy store, Le Maire, appears on the underside; from 1823 to 1860, the store was considered one of the finest in Paris, designated "as the child's Eldorado" by *Psyche* journal. In one early advertising illustration for the shop, children are shown playing with a theatre that remarkably resembles this model (see *The Encyclopedia of French Dolls* by Theimer, page 358). Excellent original condition of the rare signed room in charming petite size. $3000/4000

the doll's face is especially beautiful for this petite model. $1200/1800

87. Two Miniature Framed Prints

5" (13 cm.) x 4" larger. Two delicately-tinted engravings of aristocratic ladies of the late-18th century are presented in garland-wreathed frames. Excellent condition, one small tear in silk matting of larger frame. Late-19th century. $200/400

88. Very Rare Late-19th Century Miniature Art Nouveau Jardiniere

8" (20 cm.) Earthenware jardiniere with majolica enamel finish in shades of green, rose and cream, and in high Art Nouveau sculpting with figural face on the bowl and stylized flowers sculpted at the base of the tree-trunk-shaped pedestal. Illegible numbers incised on base with red ink mark of artist. Maker uncertain, circa 1890. Superb accessory for doll environment of great rarity and workmanship. $600/900

86. Beautiful and Rare Petite French Poupée with Sculpted Hair, with Two Early Chairs

7" (18 cm.) Bisque shoulder-head with short brown sculpted hair, painted facial features cobalt blue eyes, black upper eyeliner, accented nostrils, closed mouth, pink kid hand-stitched poupée body, wearing fine original lace gown over rose twill undergown, undergarments. Included with the doll are two fine early brass-framed chairs with original silk upholstery having needlework embroidery on seats and back. Excellent condition. French, circa 1865, rare doll and chairs in wonderfully-preserved condition,

89. French Bronze Table with Elaborate Pedestal Legs, with Porcelain Ephemera

4" (10 cm.) h. 4" table top diam. The cast bronze table has matching bronze-green marble top that is framed by a bronze filigree fringe, and rests upon a richly-shaped pedestal with center orb, and with three

gargoyle legs and claw feet. Included with the table are a pair of German bisque children statues (he holding a dog, she holding her school slate) and a porcelain-de-Paris vase with hand-painted flowers. Excellent condition. Circa 1875. $600/900

90. Very Beautiful French Bisque Poupée by Doleac in Original Summer Gown

17" (43 cm.) Bisque swivel head on kid-edged bisque shoulder plate, blue glass enamel inset eyes, dark eyeliner, lightly-feathered brows and lashes, accented nostrils and eye corners, closed mouth with accented lips, pierced ears, blonde mohair wig over cork pate, kid poupée body with gusset-jointing, stitched and separated fingers. Condition: generally excellent. Marks: L Depose 3 D. Comments: Louis Doleac, circa 1870, the facial model for his poupée was unique; he offered "undressed and dressed poupées" from his establishment at 72 Rue des Archives to luxury Parisian stores. Value Points: rare poupée with very beautiful facial model and bisque, original wig, body, and wearing her superb original two-piece summer gown of fine sheer muslin with interwoven rose ribbon bands, matching bonnet, undergarments, leather slippers, rose fingerless woven gloves. $2500/3500

91. French Bisque Poupée by Gaultier from Au Musee des Enfants with Rare Salon Chair

12" (30 cm.) Bisque swivel head on kid-edged bisque shoulder plate, blue glass enamel inset eyes, dark eyeliner, feathered brows and lashes, accented nostrils, closed mouth with center accent line, pierced ears, original blonde mohair wig over cork pate, French kid poupée body with gusset-jointing, stitched and separated fingers. Condition: generally excellent, body very sturdy. Marks: 0 (head) (original paper label of Julien Hameau of Au Musee des Enfants on torso). Comments: Gaultier, circa 1875, the poupée was costumed in the prestigious Paris boutique, Au Musee des Enfants, owned by Julien Hameau, which advertised as a maker of doll clothing, and sold in that shop, wearing its original costume. Value Points: with original shop label, the doll wears her original (faded) purple silk taffeta and velvet gown, undergarments, woven bonnet, leather heeled ankle boots, and stands beside a fine antique wooden salon chair with gold leaf finish and (frail) original silk tufted upholstery. $2200/3200

92. French All-Bisque Mignonette in Original Costume and Box

4 ½" (11 cm.) Bisque swivel head on kid-edged bisque torso, peg-jointed bisque arms and legs, dark cobalt blue glass eyes, painted features, closed mouth with gentle smile, blonde mohair wig, painted white stockings and blue two-strap heeled shoes. Condition: generally excellent. Comments: French, circa 1885. Value Points: the little girl wears her original aqua silk dress with lace edging, muslin undergarments, bonnet, and is presented in her original box with engraving of woman in a similar costume. $600/900

93. French Bisque Poupée by Gaultier in Lovely Antique Costume

22" (56 cm.) Bisque swivel head on kid-edged bisque shoulder plate, blue glass enamel inset eyes, dark eyeliner, painted features, closed mouth with center accent line, pierced ears, brunette mohair wig over cork pate, French kid gusset-jointed poupée body, stitched and separated fingers. Condition: generally excellent, very faint 1" hairline at forehead crown rim. Marks: 6 F.G. Comments: Gaultier, circa 1875. Value Points: lovely bisque and expression, beautiful spiral-threaded eyes, wearing fine antique silk costume in mauve and ivory silk, with purple velvet bonnet, undergarments, kid shoes. $1800/2800

94. Wonderful French Doll-Sized Well-Laid Banquet

17" (43 cm.) x 11"d. x 9"h. A wooden dining table with original painted finish is formally laid for a banquet for four, highlighted by a Porcelain-de-Paris dinner service including two lidded tureens, two covered casseroles, gravy boat with underplate, platter, compote, two bowls, and seven service plates, each with gold edging and floral trim; along with a blown-glass pitcher with six matching tumblers, rare cruet set with cobalt blue bottles, napkins, cutlery, champagne bottle and bucket, and plates of food highlighted by an earthenware roast turkey. Excellent condition. French, circa 1880. $900/1300

95. French Toilette Set for Bébé in Original Box with Maker's Signature

10" (25 cm.) x 7" box. A light-wooden box with decorative paper covers, silver paper borders and gilt letters "Toilette" on the lid along the maker's signature "JLP (intertwined letters) Paris Marque Depose"; the lid hinges open to reveal originally-fitted contents including porcelain wash bowl and pitcher, two matching lidded jars, various wrapped soaps, mirrors, comb, perfumes, and other accessories. Excellent condition French, circa 1890. $800/1100

96. Three French Accessories for Dolls

Including 4" carved bone folding fan with feather tips, 5" x 5" framed display of antique doll combs in various styles and sizes, and "Nouveaute de Paris" card with an assortment of objects for bébés or poupées including wrapped soaps, perfume bottle, jewelry and opera glasses. Excellent condition. French, late-19th century. $300/600

97. French Wooden Necessaire Table with Accessories

8" (20 cm.) h. closed. A wooden table with cherry finish and fancily-spindled legs, bottom shelf, beaded edging on table top, and hinges open to reveal a storage compartment that contains an assortment of fashion accessories and sewing sundries, including folding fan, muff, blue silk knit fingerless gloves, silver mesh purse, brushes, combs, scissors, thimble, heeled tan leather shoes, straw bonnet and needlework. Excellent condition. French, circa 1890. $300/600

98. Two Accessories for French Poupée

8" (20 cm.) parasol. Including a bone-handled parasol with carved detail, and having (frail) black silk cover and bone tine tips; along with a brown feather muff with padded sateen lining and brown silk fringe trim, preserved in original green cylinder box. Excellent condition except as noted. French, circa 1875. $500/700

#95

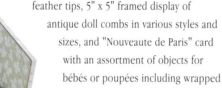
#96

#97

#98

99. Accessories for French Poupées
Including a pair of 1 ¾" soft kidskin cream slippers, and a leather box with silk lining containing two decorative faux-tortoise shell combs and a shoe-button hook. Excellent condition, silk spotted inside box. Circa 1890. $200/400

100. Two Ebony and Carved Bone Miniature Valets
6" (15 cm.) Each of the valet coat racks has wooden pedestal and stand with ebony finish, and coat arms and finial of carved bone. For display with 6"-8" dolls and their costumes. Included is an antique jacket. Circa 1885, rare. $200/400

101. French Brown Silk Gown with Velvet Trim, Mannequin Form
4 ½" (11 cm.) shoulders. To fit lady doll about 18"-20". Of a fine brown silk with narrow black interwoven stripes, the two-piece gown features a hip-length jacket over skirt with elaborately-arranged horizontal draping above a wide band of pleats at the hem, with constructed bustle at the back.

#99

#100

The jacket is trimmed with brown velvet and black cord trim, and the costume is displayed on a vintage mannequin form of wood and paper mache. Excellent condition. French, circa 1875. $400/600

102. German Wooden "Musik & Phono Handlung"
21" (53 cm.) l. x 11"h x 10"d. The wooden Art Deco era store has two front display windows, two built-in back cabinets centered by a full-length glass window with gilt lettering on the outside "Musik & Phono Handlung" (music and phonograph shop), original brown and yellow painted finish with stencil detail, original wall and floor papers, matching free-standing counter, and a hanging glass ceiling lamp. The shop is furnished with a number of miniature faux-radios and phonographs, along with a painted tin cabinet safe, and a bisque doll as shop-keeper. Very good condition. Germany, circa 1925, a rare concept shop with original gold lettering on the store window. $800/1100

103. Rare German Wooden Apothecary Shop by Moritz Gottschalk
24" (61 cm.) l. x 13"h. x 11"d. The wooden store has glass display windows at each side, and original faux-wood-grain painted finish, exterior walls and base have original pale ochre/green paint. The entire back wall has built-in shelving and cabinets, with an arched crest centering a wooden clock medallion that is attached. There are attached matching shelves on both side walls

and a free-standing matching counter. The drawers have original porcelain knobs, and painted wooden labels for various medicines and herbs. The shelves are filled with a large number of amber glass medicine bottles with original labels, wooden canisters and clear glass bottles with original labels, rare wooden barrel with original stand, various other tin and brass wear, early tin scale with brass plates and original weights, tin register, ladder, and two pairs of early dentures. A bisque dollhouse man stands in attendance. Excellent condition, the contents are rare as is the shop itself. Germany, Moritz Gottschalk, circa 1890. $2500/3500

104. Rare Grand-Sized German Wooden Dollhouse on Original Table

46" (117 cm.) h, house only. 24" h. table. 41"w. 20"d. 20"d. The two story wooden house has original painted cream finish with gold accents and lithographed paper roof. Double doors with carved valance open between the first-floor rooms, and the larger living room has a detachable sun-room at the back with valance trim to match the double doors. The kitchen is curiously placed on the second floor, as is the bathroom. Each room has original lithographed paper floor and wall papers. The house is richly furnished with antique furnishings of the era, notably red-stained parlor and bedroom set with gilt-stenciling, and a painted blue ensemble with maker's original paper label on the underside (see photo detail). Accessories include lithographed tin grandfather's clock, tin stove, porcelain clock, ceramic stove, hanging fixtures, bear rug, tin carriage, as well as many object shown in the detail photographs. Very good/excellent original condition with some typical play wear. The original table is separate and the house can be displayed with or without it. Germany, attributed to Schonherr, circa 1900. $3000/5000

#104 detail

Mark on underside of blue furniture

#104 detail

#104 detail

#104 detail

- 55 -

106. Collection of Little German Toys

9" (23 cm.) doll. Including painted composition doll with sleep eyes, with original well-detailed Scottish costume and in original Scottish box, marked A 12/0 M by Marseille; two miniature illustrated books, set of six-sided wooden blocks with scenes of children at play with dolls and toys, two Scottish terrier pups with harness. Very good/excellent condition. Circa 1900/1920. $300/500

107. German Bisque Miniature Child by K*R with Kitten

6" (15 cm.) Bisque socket head, brown glass sleep eyes, painted features, open mouth, four porcelain teeth, brunette hair wig, five-piece paper mache body with painted shoes and socks, antique silk dress and bonnet, marked 192 8/0, by Kammer and Reinhart, circa 1900. Included is a

105. German Brown-Complexioned Bisque Child by Kammer and Reinhardt

24" (62 cm.) Bisque socket head with dark brown complexion, brown glass sleep eyes, painted black lashes and brows, open mouth, four porcelain teeth, pierced ears, black human hair wig, brown composition and wooden fully-jointed body, antique costume including silk parasol. Condition generally excellent. Marks: S&H K*R 62. Comments: Kammer and Reinhardt, circa 1910. Value Points: beautiful complexion that exactly matches the original body finish. $700/1000

#108

#109

#110

fur-covered paper mache seated kitten with green glass eyes. Excellent condition. $300/500

108. German All-Bisque Doll in Presentation Box
4" (10 cm.) The all-bisque doll has one-piece head and torso, painted facial features blue eyes, blonde mohair wig, jointed arms and legs, painted pink shoes, silk costume, and is arranged in an antique box with silk cover and cast brass handle, along with additional costume pieces and a tiny doll. Doll excellent, silk of costume and box a bit worn. Germany, circa 1890. $200/400

109. German Bisque Doll with Blonde Sculpted Hair in Presentation Basket
5" (13 cm.) Bisque shoulder head with blonde sculpted hair and painted facial features, muslin body, bisque lower limbs, painted ankle boots, wearing factory-original costume and bonnet, and presented in her original woven basket with interwoven silk ribbons and silk faille lining, along with an additional bonnet, comb, and mirror. Excellent condition. Germany, circa 1880. $300/500

110. Petite German Bisque "Mein Liebling" by K*R with Vintage Miniature Christmas Tree
8" (19 cm.) Bisque socket head, blue glass set eyes, painted features, closed mouth with wistful expression, blonde mohair wig, five-piece paper mache body with painted boots, antique costume. Condition: old repair at bottom of neck socket, eyes set, body not original. Marks: K*R Simon & Halbig 117/A 19. Comments: Kammer and Reinhardt, circa 1912, their "Mein Liebling" model. Value Points: sought-after model, she is posed alongside her vintage German Christmas tree with original wooden stand, decorated with glass balls and tiny candles that are original on little brass spirals. $1200/1800

111. French Paper Mache Candies in Original Boxes with Basket and Tea Set
7" (18 cm.) basket. A finely-woven oval basket with tufted silk lining contains a miniature porcelain tea service for four (creamer handle broken). Along with a beautiful box "Violettes pralines" with its original arrangement of paper mache candies and treats, and with another box with lithograph of lilies of the valley on the lid and paper mache treats inside. Excellent condition except as noted. Circa 1890. $300/500

112. French Earthenware Toy Dishes with Paper Mache Food in Original Box
10" (25 cm.) x 9" box. 3" plate diam. Still attached inside the original card stock box is an earthenware service with sponge-pattern green/ochre design, comprising four plates and one bowl, each containing a paper mache delicacy or fruit, along with a cake plate with berry-trimmed cake, and with four cotton print napkins, and four spoons. Excellent condition. French, circa 1910. $300/500

113. German Porcelain Miniature Tea Set with Figural Woman
5" (13 cm.) h. teapot. The porcelain tea set features a lidded pot, sugar and creamer in the shape of a plump woman with sculpted hair and painted facial features, along with four cups and saucers with tulip design. Excellent condition. Germany, circa 1920. $200/300

114. Wonderful German Tea Room with Pastry Shop
31" (79 cm.) l. x 14"h x 16"d. The wooden framed store has original cream painted finish with gold accents to simulate architectural details, with attached front railing having metal grillwork and window boxes. The back wall has built in shelves, upper railing for display, center display

niche and window cabinets at each side. The floor and wall paper are original, and there is a free-standing matching counter. The shop is lavishly-filled with wonderful pastries and baked goods, most on their original wooden pedestal cake stands, and a rare three-tiered wooden etagere on the counter holds more pastries. There are two tables and chairs for customers to take tea as they gaze out over the window boxes. Other furnishings include: pair of gilded metal oil lamps, wooden wall rack filled with miniature newspapers and menu cards, framed prints including advertising scene for Stollwerck's Chocolates, coat rack, samovar, tin "Eismachine" and cash register with rare attached paper roll. A blonde-haired store keeper stands behind the counter. Excellent condition. Germany, circa 1900. $2500/3500

116. French Porcelain-de-Paris Dinner Service in Original Box

13" (33 cm.) x 10" box. The cardboard box with decorative paper cover contains its original porcelain doll-sized service, with pink shaded borders, gold rims, and garlands of colorful flowers, comprising 3" lidded tureen, oval platter, bowl, square sauce bowl, gravy boat, handled relish dish, and eight shallow bowls. Porcelain excellent, box worn. French, circa 1885. $400/600

117. French Faience Service in Original Box by Cuperly, Blondel & Gerbeau

15" (38 cm.) x 9" box. 4" carafe. A light-wood box with Art Nouveau decorative paper covers has original label on lid "Service Faience, Fabrique Francaise, CBG" with references to Medaille'Or awards at the 1889 International Exposition. The box hinges open to reveal well-fitted contents, primarily creamy faience with designs of flowers and leaves encircles, by blue and gold borders, along with rare teal blue glassware comprising two footed compotes, carafe, four goblets, serving plate and two small bowls, with cutlery, napkins, and menu cards. Very good, unplayed with condition items still tied with rose silk ribbons in original box, albeit a bit dusty, few minor rough edges on glassware. Cuperly, Blondel & Gerbeau, circa 1890. $500/800

115. French Wooden Cupboard with Painted Decorations and Faience Dinner Ware

22" (56 cm.) The wooden cabinet is painted original pale-apple-green with cream panels decorated with floral designs and gilt edging, and is filled with a creamy faience doll-sized dinner ware service with pink and blue flowers and green trailing vines and leaves, comprising two lidded tureens, lidded sauce dish, gravy boat, two handled relish dishes, platter, compote, two oval sauce dishes, 12 various plates, and two large round serving dishes. Excellent condition. French, circa 1890. $700/1100

118. German Wooden Candy Shop with Awnings by Gottschalk

21" (53 cm.) l. x 13"h. x 9"d. The wooden framed store has unusual open sides with scallop-shaped shelving that is accessible from both the sides and front. The front counter is attached to the two tall cabinets on either side, and there is a wall of built-in shelving at the back wall with eight spice drawers having porcelain labels and porcelain knobs, a center display niche with mirrored back and several open shelves. The green painted finish is edged with cream and accented with gold columns, and there is a cloth awning at each of the windows. The shop is well-laden with candy jars, candies, dishes of treats, cast iron scale and other accessories, and there is a bisque head lady with pale blonde hair in attendance. Germany, attributed to Gottschalk, circa 1915. $1100/1800

119. German Porcelain Hot Chocolate Service

7" (18 cm.) tray. 1 ¾"h. cups. Of white porcelain with scalloped edges and decorative transfer designs of cupids at play, the service comprises an unusual tray and three cups, the cups designed to rest inside the column openings, and the tray designed for cookies or sweets. Excellent condition, one cup lacking. Germany, circa 1890. $100/300

120. German Porcelain Hot Chocolate Service with Cupid Theme

6" (15 cm.) tray. 1 ¾" cup. Of white porcelain with pink shaded borders and designs of frolicking cupids, the service comprises a tray and six mugs with gold-accented handles. Excellent condition. Germany, circa 1890. $200/400

121. Pair, French Bisque Bride and Groom by Gaultier with Original Costumes

11" (28 cm.) Each has bisque swivel head on kid-edged bisque shoulder plate, blue glass enamel inset eyes, painted lashes and brows, closed mouth, pierced ears, blonde mohair wig over cork pate, kid poupée body with kid arms. Condition: generally excellent, bride's gown frail. Marks: 3/0 (head) F.G. 3/0 (shoulders). Comments: Gaultier, circa 1887; beneath the original costumes, the doll bodies are wrapped in old French newspapers dated 1887. Value Points: the pair of petite poupées are wearing their original bride and groom wedding costumes. $2000/3000

122. Rare Set of French Bronze Salon Furnishings

5 ½" (14 cm.) h. 7"l. settee. Having cast bronze frames with ornate detailing suggestive of the Louis XVI era, and with silk upholstered seats and backs, the extensive 13-piece salon set comprises ten side chairs, one arm chair, settee, and a table with gilt metallic trim. Excellent condition. French, mid-19th century, perfect for slightly-larger dollhouse room, or with 4"-6" mignonettes. Rare and extensive set is virtually unfindable. $500/800

123. French All-Bisque Mignonette with Painted Brown Boots in Wicker Egg Presentation

6" (15 cm.) doll. 9"l. egg. Solid-domed bisque swivel head on kid-edged bisque torso, cobalt blue glass enamel inset eyes, dark eyeliner, painted lashes and brows, accented nostrils, closed mouth with center accent line, blonde mohair wig, peg-jointed bisque arms and legs with painted white stockings and brown ankle boots. Condition: generally excellent. Comments: French, circa 1880. Value Points: very beautiful all-bisque doll in rare larger size, rich cobalt eyes, rare brown boots, original wig, antique silk costume, and presented in antique French woven egg-shaped basket with silk lining, and various added accessories. $900/1600

124. Petite French 19th Century Opera with Rare Theatre Dolls

17" (43 cm.) x 13". The wooden theatre with original cream and gold paint and red banner with gold "Opera" lettering, has marble-paper covered base and set-back stage, with candelabra and four bisque theatre dolls, each with bisque shoulder head, glass inset eyes, painted features, closed mouth, mohair wig, bisque lower limbs, original silk costumes of Louis XVI era, and details of accessories including the lady's wig in the style of Marie Antoinette. Very good condition, theatre original, bisque excellent, costumes and wigs are original albeit quite frail. French, circa 1890, the German-made dolls costumed for the theatre and rare to find with these costumes. $1700/2500

125. Two Framed Portraits in Decorative Frames
4" (10 cm.) x 4" largest. Images of two 18th century ladies include a woman in country costume leaning against her horse, and an aristocratic lady in elaborate hat and blue gown, each in decorative frame to simulate marble. Excellent condition, age uncertain. $200/400

126. Petite English Porcelain Tea Service for Two
7" (18 cm.) l. tray. 2"h. teapot. The porcelain tray with gold edging is decorated with dainty colorful pansies and roses, and holds a tea service for two with matching designs, comprising lidded teapot, lidded sugar, creamer, two cups and saucers; the service is enhanced by the unusual turquoise handles of each piece. Marked "Crown Staffordshire England A.D. 1801" with symbol of crown. Excellent condition. $300/500

127. French Blown Glass Miniature Decanter Set
4" (10 cm.) diam. tray. 3" decanter. A blown glass circular tray with gilt edging and blue bead decorations holds a matching service comprising decanter with gold-tipped stopper, four tumblers, and a lidded jar. Excellent condition. French, circa 1890. $300/500

128. Two Miniature Bisque Curio Shelves with Bisque Cupid Ornamentation
3" (8 cm.) The matched pair of curio shelves, in the Louis XVI style, have gold finish with gold decorative glaze at the edges, and are decorated with sculpted bisque winged cupids. Excellent condition. Germany, circa 1890. $200/400

128.1. French Accessories for Poupées

4" (10 cm.) l. umbrella. Including a wooden-handled black-cotton umbrella (one edge worn), a leather valise with purple silk lining, and an oval wooden hat box with original leather straps containing black velvet bonnet. Very good/excellent condition. French, circa 1880, for display with larger poupées. $400/600

129. Petite French Bisque Poupée by Gaultier, Size 0, in Original Costume

12" (30 cm.) Bisque swivel head on kid-edged bisque shoulder plate, blue glass enamel inset eyes, painted lashes and brows, accented nostrils, closed mouth with accented lips, pierced ears, blonde mohair wig over cork pate, French kid gusset-jointed body, stitched and separated fingers. Condition: generally excellent. Marks: 0. Comments: Gaultier, circa 1875. Value Points: the petite poupée, size 0, with original wig, wears her (somewhat frail) original two-piece gown with black lace trim, bone-handled parasol with silk fringe, bonnet, undergarments, leather ankle boots signed 0. $2200/2800

130. Superb Burled Walnut Doll-Sized Grandfather Clock

21" (53 cm.) The tall case (Grandfather) clock is of fine burled walnut with superb cabinetry and design, heightened by bronze mounts and finials, with decorative silver and brass face having surmounting astronomical designs. The clock is activated by keywind at the back. The clockworks are stamped "Echappement ancre, 7 rubis, made in France", and "Bayard" (in circle). Excellent condition. Mid-20th century. $800/1200

#133 with cover

#133 without cover

131. Pair, French Salon Chairs with Burgundy Silk Tufted Upholstery

9" (23 cm.) The matched pair of side chairs are richly upholstered in burgundy silk with detail of tufting on the back and seat, and trimmed with ivory cord and ivory silk fringe. Excellent condition. French, late-19th century. $500/800

132. French Paper Mache Borzoi Salon Dog

8" (20 cm.) Very slender paper mache Borzoi dog is lavishly covered with white fur except shaved legs and face, brown velvet ears, glass bead eyes, open mouth. Excellent condition. French, circa 1900. $300/500

133. French Leather Necessaire for Poupée with Original Canvas Cover

6" (15 cm.) A firm-sided red leather valise with brass lock and key, leather bail handle and fitted interior containing 2 brushes, comb, and four sewing tools, is preserved in its original traveling canvas cover. A rare accessory, perfectly sized for display with 20"-22" poupée or smaller bébé, and perfectly preserved including rare cover. Excellent condition. French, circa 1875. $800/1200

133.1. German Ormolu Dollhouse Furnishings and Decorations

6" (15 cm.) h. fireplace. Each of fine richly-gilded ormolu including fireplace with fender, mantel and mirror; four various frames with mirrors or prints, table top lamp, and a floor lamp with glass bead drops and milk glass shade. Along with three ormolu valances (with curtains, not original); and with two wooden-pot with gilt paper trim containing silk rose plants. Excellent condition. Circa 1890. $600/900

134. Petite French Bisque Poupée by Gaultier in Original Silk Gown

11" (28 cm.) Bisque swivel head on kid-edged bisque shoulder plate, blue glass enamel inset eyes, painted lashes, feathered

brows, accented nostrils, closed mouth with accent line between the lips, pierced ears, brunette mohair wig over cork pate, French kid poupée body with shapely torso and legs, stitched and separated fingers. Condition: generally excellent. Marks: 2/0. Comments: Gaultier, circa 1870. Value Points: all-original condition of the rare petite poupée with beautiful original gown and matching bonnet, undergarments, leather shoes marked 2/0. $1800/2600

135. Fine French Curio Cabinet with Bronze Trim, with Miniature Statuary and Accessories

11" (28 cm.) Rosewood vitrine with fine detail of cabinetry including beautifully-chosen burled veneer woods, cast bronze braid decoration framing the window front and forming medallions, with cascading garlands at the sides and bronze edging at the top. With lock and key, and velvet-lined interior. The cabinet is a classic example of the superb luxury goods of Maison Giroux & Cie, the mid-19th century decorative arts store which also presented fine accessories for poupées. The cabinet has a collection of eight tiny bisque and porcelain statues of children and ladies, and a clock with marble crest and base and two painted vases adorn the cabinet top. Excellent condition. Circa 1870. $1200/1600

136. German Mechanical Fluttering Bird by Bing

7" (18 cm.) h. bird cage. A metal birdcage with painted red tin base resting on painted gold tin acanthus legs, encloses a tin bird with beautifully-painted details of feathers, perched upon a tin plant. When wound, from hidden mechanism below, the bellows opens and closes, and the bird nods back and forth as though flapping its wings. Included with the cage is a 7"h. French wooden table. Excellent condition. Germany, attributed to Bing $400/600

137. French Paper Mache Cat as Candy Container

7" (18 cm.) The paper mache cat with white fur cover has shaved legs and face, blue glass eyes, ears, and fluffy tail. The head removes for its original use as candy container. Excellent condition. French, circa 1890. $300/500

138. French Bisque Early Poupée with Cobalt Blue Eyes by Gaultier

13" (33 cm.) Bisque shoulder head with very plump face, cobalt blue glass enamel eyes, painted features, closed mouth with center accent line, unpierced ears, blonde mohair wig over cork pate, shapely kid poupée body, stitched and separated fingers, wearing antique dress, undergarments, stockings, shoes and woven bonnet. Condition: generally excellent. Marks: F. 1 G. Comments: Gaultier, circa 1865. Value Points: wonderful expression enhanced by fine bisque and brilliant eyes. $1200/1700

139. Early-20th Century Doll-Sized Oak Bedroom Ensemble with Marble Tops

22" (56 cm.) h. canopy bed. Of dark-stained oak in the Arts and Crafts style, with incised carving of flowers, the set comprises canopy bed with lace and silk bed covers; 16" chest of drawers with mirror and marble top; 18" armoire with richly-detailed carving, and two 7" night stands with white marble tops. Included is a porcelain wash bowl and pitcher in rich cobalt blue with gold accents. Maker uncertain, European, circa 1900. Excellent condition. $400/600

140. French Porcelain Dinner Service with Rare Pressed Glass Compotes

6" (15 cm.) h. tureen. Of fine white porcelain with blue and gold striped designs, the service comprises a rare lattice-design fruit bowl, along with three lidded tureens, two compotes, eight various plates and shallow bowls. Along with a pair of exquisite aqua glass footed compotes with pressed pattern designs. Excellent condition. French, circa 1880. $300/500

141. French Toy Horse and Cart
10" (25 cm.) A carved wooden horse with original dappled brown hide cover has amber glass eyes and original leather harness, mane, tail, and is attached to a woven cart with two metal spoked wheels, wooden seat and baggage compartment that opens and closes. Beautifully-preserved condition of the fine quality toy in rare size. French, circa 1880. $500/800

142. German Bisque Character, 444, by Bahr and Proschild in Original Costume
10" (25 cm.) Bisque socket head, blue glass sleep eyes, painted features, open mouth, four porcelain teeth, brunette mohair wig, Sonneberg composition and wooden fully-jointed body. Condition: generally excellent. Marks: 444 4/0. Comments: Bahr and Proschild, circa 1890. Value Points: rare model wearing his original linen suit, red flannel vest, leather ankle boots, brown felt cape, brown velvet cap. $500/800

143. German Bisque Child on Sled as Candy Container
4 ½" (11 cm.) seated. A bisque head doll with blue glass eyes, painted features, open mouth, teeth, blonde mohair wig, carton hollow torso that separates at the waist for use as candy container, paper mache lower arms and legs, is wearing his factory original knit suit and cap, and is seated upon a wooden sled. Excellent condition. Germany, circa 1910, all-original and well-preserved. $600/900

144. A Plentifully-Filled German Wooden Toy Store by Gottschalk
13" (33 cm.) h. x 20"l. x 8"d. A wooden store with display cabinets at both sides of the open front has arched pediment trim, a fitted back display cabinet with open shelves and free-standing counter. The store has original cream painted finish with blue stencil trim, lithographed-paper on exterior, and

original wall and floor paper inside. The shelves are filled to overflowing with toys, dolls and other playthings including rolly-dolly, bisque dolls (several in original boxes), Erzebirge wooden figures and vehicles, paper mache horses, paper clown face with pull-string tongue, wooden skis, carved wooden nutcracker soldiers, bisque Polichinelle, rocking horses, lead soldiers, teddy bears, snow baby, miniature blocks in original box, and much more. Two bisque dolls stand behind the counter. Excellent condition, finish on store wood is original albeit rubbed. Gottschalk, circa 1900, a fabulous store with seemingly-endless little treasures. $3500/5500

146. Collection of Vintage Photographs of Children with Dolls and Toys
Mostly about 4" x 2 ½". Fourteen vintage studio photographs on cardboard backing depict children of late-19th/early-20th century posed with playthings; one group of six cards from the Henri Becker Studio of Brussels appears to depict all the children in one family (six boys and one girl!) each posed with a hoop. Five photographs depict girls holding their dolls, and three photos feature children on toy horses. Excellent condition. Circa 1890/1900. $300/600

147. Two Rare Early Tinplate Miniatures
3" (8 cm.) table. Each of pressed tinplate, including rare game table with printed paper cover featuring wood grain around the table top edge centers a checkerboard center; and a desk inkwell with original red paint, gold stenciled design, and feather quill. Excellent condition. Mid-19th century, very rare. $300/600

148. Tiny Early Flip Book and Ephemera
1 ¼" (3 cm.) A paper-covered miniature book is designed with black and white images on the interior, designed so when pages are quickly flipped, the images appear to move (much in the manner of early film). Along with a rare pair of celluloid (bakelite?) opera glasses with blurred Stanhope-like images of German scenes. Excellent condition. Early 20th century. $200/300

145. Seven German Miniature Wooden Blocks in Original Boxes
2" (5 cm.) x 1 ½". Seven cardboard boxes with different colorful lithographs on the lids depicting children playing, are each fitted with a set of six wooden blocks. Each set of blocks is six-sided, allowing for the possibility of different images to be constructed, and each box also contains miniature lithographs of the puzzles within. Near mint condition and very rare to find in this tiny size. Germany, circa 1910. $300/600

149. Collection of 32 French Trade Cards of Children with Dolls and Toys
4" (10 cm.) x 2 ½". Each card features children of 1885 era at play with their toys, mostly stylishly-dressed little girls with their dolls. The cards were printed from original miniature oil paintings by artist Luigi Loir and others, and each features advertising for chocolates, tapioca, or other treats. Excellent condition, one corner torn. French, circa 1885. $300/400

150. Rare French Bisque Automaton "Little Girl Crying for Her Broken Polichinelle" by Lambert

19" (48 cm.) Standing upon a velvet-covered wooden platform is a bisque-head girl with highly-characterized crying expression, narrow blue glass eyes as though squinting through tears, painted lashes and brows, accented nostrils of rounded nose, closed mouth modeled as though open in wide crying expression, sculpted upper teeth and tongue, applied tears under each eye, pierced ears, brunette mohair wig over cork pate, French carton torso and legs, bisque forearms, original silk and lace costume with matching bonnet. She is holding a bisque-head Polichinelle in her right hand, with his body dangling below as though he is broken, and a hankie in her left hand. When wound, music plays, she lifts the Polichinelle as though to show the tragedy that has befallen her favorite toy, then drops it again, and turns to her left hand, lifts the hankie as though to wipe away her tears. Condition: generally excellent, mechanism and music function well, costume a bit frail. Marks: 211 (head) L.B. (key), and original paper tune label with ink-script name of music, "Bal chez le Ministre". Comments: Leopold Lambert, with bisque head especially commissioned for the automaton from Jumeau, circa 1890. Value Points: rare automaton with most endearing and realistic scene, rare character head, beautiful bisque, original tears. $8000/12,000

151. Collection of French Postcards of Children with Dolls
5" (13 cm.) x 3". Forty-two photographic postcards feature images of children at play, mostly girls with dolls; included are several series including the delightful "Bal, Mariage, and Bapteme" series of Polichinelle and Bébé Jumeau. Good to excellent condition. French, late-19th century. $200/300

152. Set of Early Engravings of Child with Doll
6" (15 cm.) x 5" framed. The set of six frames features delicately-colored illustrations of a young girl tenderly at play with her doll, in various scenes, framed to match. Good condition, some spotting. French, circa 1840. $200/400

153. Early German Convent School Room with Attached Nun's Room and Rare Accessories
31" (79 cm.) l. x 14"h. x 15"d. A wooden framed doll house with arched back windows and lithographed exterior papers features two rooms, each with original floor and wall papers. The larger room is the classroom, with wooden desks and benches for six students, each with porcelain inkwell and porcelain hat hook, teacher's desk with platform base, wooden easel with slate, shelving, fold-over ladder, bench and stoneware stove. Seated at the desks are six all-bisque students with glass eyes, mohair wigs, wearing school uniforms. Each student owns a notebook with decoupage decoration on the cover, a wooden pencil case and a leatherette satchel. There is an abacus, globe, wall clock, mathematical tools, and a collection of paper mache animals for study. A wax nun in original habit stands at the front of class. Behind the nun is a door opening to her small room which is fitted with a bed, cabinet of linens, table with artifacts, rare lace-making board, and framed prints. Room has original papers in worn condition, contents are excellent. Germany, circa 1890. $3000/4000

- 75 -

capelet collar and embroidery. Mostly excellent albeit dusty, two silk pieces frail. Circa 1890. $300/600

155. Delightful French "Lady with Baby in Carriage" Mechanical Toy by Vichy

12" (30 cm.) l. 9"h. lady. A bisque head lady with blue glass eyes, painted lashes and brows, closed mouth with accented lips, pierceé ears, blonde mohair wig over cork pate, carton torso, metal hands and legs, is clasping the handle of a metal carriage with filigree sides, and three spoked wheels; an all-bisque mignonette baby rests in the carriage, having cobalt blue glass enamel eyes, painted features, closed mouth, original blonde mohair wig, peg-jointed bisque arms and legs painted shoes. When keywound, the lady moves her legs forward and back as though walking, and propels the carriage forward. Condition: generally excellent. Comments: Vichy, circa 1875. Value Points: the charming vignette mechanical toy is all-original, the lady with (dusty) peach silk frock and bonnet, and the baby in original long gown with lace trim. $3500/5500

154. Miniature Costumes in Original Boxes from Old Store Stock

5" (13 cm.) x 2 ½" boxes. Simple cardboard boxes (worn, and two lacking lids) contain costumes for mignonettes or dollhouse dolls, including mostly blouses and little dresses, one set of undergarments with matching lace, and a beautiful white pique cape with

156. Set of Miniature Fashion Folios in Original Book Box

4" (10 cm.) x 3". A book box titled "La Mode Feminine de 1795 a 1900" contains four folios, each with 20 heavy stock cards having illustrations of fashions from a particular era of history, from Editions Nilsson, Paris. (Folios excellent, book box worn). Along with 13 fashion engravings, 5 ½" x 3", depicting costumes of the 1840 era, in fair/good condition. $200/400

157. Wonderful Tiny German Wooden Milliner's Shop by Christian Hacker
13" (33 cm.) x 10"h. x 7"d. The wooden shop with original ochre paint and green trim has hinged front display windows with shelving that can swing open for play, shelving and display niches against the back wall, original wall and floor papers and a matching free-standing counter. The shop is fitted with fabric, laces, trims, buttons, 11 miniature bonnets, umbrella stand with three bone-handled faux parasols, chrystal chandelier, purses, and a glass chandelier. A china head doll-house doll stands in attendance. The shop name "Parifer Moden" (Parisian Mode) appears above the front windows. Excellent condition. Germany, Christian Hacker, circa 1880, very rare tiny size. $1200/1700

158. Three 19th Century Doll-Sized Accessories

5" (13 cm.) mirror. Including cast brass hand mirror with very ornate frame having figural head of a lady at the center crest, velvet-covered book box containing an enamel-back faux watch on brooch pin, and a miniature painting of aristocratic lady signed by artist (Hermu?) in walnut oval frame. Excellent condition. 19th century. $300/500

159. Beautiful French Bisque Waltzing Lady by Vichy

18" (46 cm.) The bisque head lady with swivel head on bisque shoulder plate has blue glass enamel eyes, painted features, closed mouth, pierced ears, blonde mohair wig over cork pate, carton torso and legs, metal hands, and is posed standing upon a metal wheeled base that is hidden by her skirt. When wound, she glides forward, then twirls to the side, then repeats in a graceful manner, while meanwhile she alternately fans herself or gazes in the mirror. Condition: generally excellent, mechanism functions well, costume is original albeit spotted and a bit frail. Comments: Vichy, circa 1870. Value Points: the prestige luxurious automaton has elegant movements and wears her original costume. $6000/9500

160. Rare French Decorative Accessories for Poupée

3" (8 cm.) pair vases. Included is a pair of blue blown glass mantel vases with gold edging and beaded floral designs, superb 2¼" porcelain bowl in ormolu pedestal frame and having unusual matte finish with exuberantly-painted wild flowers on the interior bowl; and 3" blue glass plate in ormolu frame and pedestal base, with deeply-cut etched design of woman and cupid on plate. Excellent condition. French, circa 1875. $500/800

161. French Porcelain Toilette Ensemble and Gloves

4" (10 cm.) h. bowl. Of fine white porcelain with raised designs and decorated with shaded blue background framed with garlands of rose buds, and gold edging, including wash bowl and pitcher, lidded box, lidded bowl, and open bowl. Along with two blue glass toilette bottles with white enamel decorations, bone-tipped powder puff, and a pair of cream leather gloves. French, circa 1885. Excellent condition. $300/600

162. Beautiful French Bisque Poupée, Size 0, by Gaultier

12" (30 cm.) Bisque swivel head on kid-edged bisque shoulder plate, blue glass enamel inset eyes, dark eyeliner, painted lashes and brows, accented nostrils and eye corners, closed mouth with center accent line, pierced ears, blonde mohair wig, ears pierced into head, blonde mohair wig over cork pate, French kid poupée body with gusset-jointing, stitched and separated fingers. Condition: generally excellent. Marks: 0 (head) F.G. 0 (shoulders). Comments: Gaultier, circa 1870. Value Points: an especially beautiful early model by Gaultier with delicate bisque, wearing fine antique costume, original wig. $2000/3000

#166.1

163. Rare French Bisque Automaton Toy by Roullet et Decamps
16" (41 cm.) The toy features two bisque-head dolls, each with amber-tinted complexion, black glass eyes, painted black brows and lashes, open mouth, four porcelain teeth, black mohair wig, carton torso and legs, bisque forearms, wearing original silk Japanese costumes. One doll is standing in front of a wooden cart as though pulling it, and the other is sitting in the cart. When wound, he walks briskly forward, and she urges him on, waving her arms. Condition: generally excellent, mechanism functions well, one finger chipped on body. Marks: 1079 -2 Dep S&H Germany (boy) 1079-3/0 Dep S&H Germany (girl). Comments: Roullet et Decamps, circa 1910. Value Points: a rare variation of their popular cart series. $1800/2500

164. German Bisque Asian Baby by Marseille in Wonderful Costume
12" (30 cm.) Solid domed bisque socket head with amber-tinted complexion, black painted hair and brows, tiny brown glass sleep eyes, painted lashes, closed mouth with downcast lips, amber-tinted composition baby body. Condition: generally excellent. Marks: 2 Germany. Comments: Marseille, circa 1920. Value Points: the pouty-faced model of Asian baby wears wonderful antique kimono and cap. $400/600

165. German Bisque Asian Baby with Rare Glazed Complexion
12" (30 cm.) Solid domed bisque socket head with richly-tinted amber complexion that is heightened by decorative glaze, black tinted hair and brows, tiny brown glass sleep eyes, painted lashes, closed mouth, amber-tinted composition baby body, wearing antique kimono and pants. Marks: 0 Germany. Comments: Germany, circa 1920. Value Points: well-detailed sculpting includes indentations at outside corners of narrow eyes, plump cheeks, beautiful complexion. $400/600

166. German Bisque Asian Child in Fine Silk Costume
11" (28 cm.) Amber-tinted bisque socket head, brown glass inset eyes, painted lashes and brows, accented nostrils, slightly-parted lips, four porcelain teeth, pierced ears, black mohair wig, amber-tinted composition and wooden fully-jointed body. Condition: generally excellent. Marks: 4/0. Comments: Germany, circa 1885. Value Points: fine deep sculpting details, original body and body finish wearing beautiful antique silk gown with embroidered details. $800/1000

166.1. Two French All-Bisque Asian Dolls
2 ½" (6 cm.) Each is all-bisque with amber-tinted complexion, swivel head, painted facial features, peg-jointed bisque arms and legs, black mohair wig or queue, and wearing original costume, preserved in early box. Excellent condition. French, circa 1890. $200/400

167. 19th Century Silk Costume for Asian Doll with Mirror
To fit about 20" child doll. 5" shoulder width, 12" costume length. Of natural silk in rich mustard color, the tunic has cotton lining, wing-like sleeves and is richly embroidered overall. Included with an ebony Psyche mirror with mother-of-pearl inlay in frame, and hinged mirror with beveled glass, and with a single Chinese shoe for larger child doll. Very good condition. Late-19th century. $300/500

stamp, and impressed "Wedgewood". Excellent except as noted. Mid-19th century. $300/500

170. A Trio of German Bisque Miniature Dolls with Unusual Variations

4" (10 cm.) Each has bisque socket head with amber tinted complexion and painted facial features, brown eyes, closed mouth, arched brows, amber-tinted five-piece paper mache body with painted pointy-toe slippers, wearing antique costume. Condition: generally excellent. Comments: Germany, probably Simon & Halbig, circa 1890. Value Points: fascinating study of three dolls that are identical with variation in hair style: one with painted pate and mohair queue, one with bald pate and mohair queue, and the third with an elaborately-arranged coiffure ornamented with beads and ormolu. $800/1200

168. Extensive French Child-sized Dinner Service with Brown Floral Design

6" (15 cm.) h. tureen. Of creamy softpaste with delicate design of mauve flowers and trailing brown vines, accented with gold borders, the service comprises large lidded tureen, rare large lidded footed tureen with underplate, three casserole or vegetable lidded bowls, three oval platters, square bread plate, gravy boat with attached underplate, four small relish dishes, six shallow soup bowls, six dessert plates, and twelve large dinner plates. Excellent condition. French, circa 1875, a very extensive service including several rare pieces. $300/600

169. English Child's Soft-Paste Wedgewood Service with Rare Dragon Theme

4 ½" (11 cm.) l. tureen. The creamy soft-paste dinner service is decorated with geometric-patterned black border and decorated with green Chinese dragons, the set comprising large lidded tureen, smaller lidded tureen (lid reglued), lidded casserole with underplate, gravy boat with underplate, six shallow bowls or plates, and two oval platters. The set is marked "Wedgewood Etruria England" in black

171. Pair, German Bisque Asian Children, 1129, by Simon and Halbig in Matching Antique Costumes

7" (18 cm.) and 8". Each has bisque socket head with amber-tinted

- 82 -

complexion, brown glass inset eyes in narrow side-slant sockets, black single stroke arched brows, painted lashes, open mouth, four tiny teeth, black mohair wig, the larger with amber-tinted composition and wooden ball-jointed body, the smaller with five-piece body. Condition: generally excellent. Marks: 1129 Germany Simon & Halbig S&H. Comments: Simon and Halbig, circa 1900. Value Points: beautiful little pair with lovely bisque and sculpting, wearing matching silk costumes with embroidered details. Included is a Chinese wooden lacquered cabinet. $1200/1500

#172

#173

172. Very Fine French Sevres Miniature Porcelain Tête-à-Tête
7" (18 cm.) l. tray. 2"h. teapot. Of fine white porcelain with painted pink background enhanced with gold borders and gold stars, and with medallions of colorful floral clusters on each piece, comprising large tray, lidded teapot, creamer, lidded sugar, and two cups and saucers. With Sevres blue stamp. Excellent condition. French, circa 1875, perfect for display with 17"-20" poupée. $300/400

173. French Porcelain Tête-à-Tête with Colorful Floral Decorations
3" (8 cm.) Of fine quality white porcelain the tea set is designed with beautifully-shaped pots and scalloped-edge tray, having gold-leaf borders, and transfer decorations of colorful bouquets of wild flowers, comprising lidded teapot, lidded sugar, creamer, two cups and saucers, two spoons, and tray. Excellent condition. French, circa 1880, a very delicately-patterned dainty service for two. $300/500

174. French Porcelain Doll's Dinner Service in Rare Colors
4 ½" (11 cm.) lidded tureen. Of fine white porcelain with pale yellow painted borders edged with gold trim, and decorated with blue flowers and leaves, the service comprises a lidded tureen, footed compote, ladle, square serving dish with lid, vegetable bowl, gravy boat with attached underplate, handled relish dish, oval platter, large serving plate, six dinner plates, and six dessert plate. Excellent condition. French, circa 1875, rare and complete set with beautiful colors. $400/500

175. French Porcelain-de-Paris Tête-à-Tête
2 ½" (6 cm.) Of fine white porcelain with coral highlights and transfer decorations of cherry blossoms and leaves, including round tray, lidded pot, lidded sugar, creamer, two cups and saucers. Excellent condition. French, circa 1890. $300/400

176. Rare and Exquisite French Bisque Automaton "The Chinese Tea Server" with Original Lambert Paper Label
19" (48 cm.) Standing upon a velvet-covered base is a bisque-head lady with amber-tinted complexion enhancing her angular heart-shaped face, narrow brown glass

#174

inset eyes, dark eyeliner, long painted brown lashes and thick brows, accented nostrils, closed mouth with very full lips, pierced ears, black mohair wig in upswept fashion over cork pate, slender carton torso and legs, wire upper arms, amber-tinted bisque forearms. When wound, the lady elegantly turns her head side to side, then inclines her head as though offering tea, she lifts the tea pot and, in a refined and gracious manner, pours the tea into a cup on the tray she holds, then extends the tray as though serving. Music plays throughout. Condition: generally excellent, mechanism and music function well, costume a bit dusty. Marks: (original tune label "Carmen" on underside) L. Lambert Fabricant Objets Automatiques Articles Riche 13 Rue Portefoin (original gilt lettered red paper label on underside). Comments: Leopold Lambert, circa 1888, with bisque head commissioned from Jumeau and sculpted exclusively for this luxury automaton model. Value Points: rare model with superb facial model, lovely bisque, very refined movements, wearing her original gold silk and velvet costume (an identically-costumed model is shown in *The Encyclopedia of French Dolls* by Theimer, page 337), and with very rare original Lambert paper label. $8000/12,000

#175

#177 detail

177. French Child-Sized Porcelain "Rosebud" Dinner Service

6" (15 cm.) h. tureen. Of fine white porcelain with painted pale blue background and decorated with dainty rosebuds, ferns and vines, with gilt accents and finials, the service comprises lidded tureen, bowl, footed compote, round serving platter, oval platter, covered vegetable dish, gravy boat, relish dish, six dinner plates and six soup bowls. French, circa 1885. Excellent condition, exquisite quality of decoration details. $400/600

178. 19th Century Accessories for Larger Poupées or Bébés

17" (43 cm.) tree. Comprising a woven wicker chair with tufted burgundy silk seat; paper mache salon dog with fur cover and amber glass eyes, in rare resting pose; and a vintage Christmas tree with wooden base, decorated with textured silver balls and with garlands of silver balls in graduated sizes. Very good/ excellent condition. Circa 1890. $700/1100

179. Early-20th Century Art Nouveau Folding Screen with Hand-Painted Designs

23" (58 cm.) Having dark oak frame, the four-panel folding screen has opaque glass panels with hand-painted floral and foliage scenes. Excellent condition. Circa 1900. $300/600

179.1. French Burled Walnut Doll-Sized Chest of Maitrise Quality

9" (23 cm.) The maitrise-quality chest of three drawers has superb cabinetry work, with dove-tailed drawers, voluptuously-curved bombe front, shaped top surface and finest burled veneers, and is fitted with cast iron elaborate drawer pulls, keys holes (key not included) and trim. Excellent condition. French, circa 1880, in the 18th century style, probably Maison Giroux of Paris. $600/900

180. Large French Bisque Poupée by Gaultier with Rare Gesland Body

24" (61 cm.) Bisque swivel head on kid-edged bisque shoulder plate, blue glass enamel inset eyes with spiral threading, dark eyeliner, painted lashes, and brows, rose blushed eye shadow, accented nostrils, closed mouth with accented lips, pierced ears, blonde mohair wig over cork pate, French padded stockinette body with metal armature allowing posing, bisque hands, lower legs and bare feet, wearing original undergarments and cap, and antique gown is included. Condition: generally excellent, chip on neck rim of shoulder-plate at back, body especially sturdy with perfect bisque limbs. Marks: 7 F. G (doll) (partial Gesland stamp on body). Comments: Gaultier, circa 1875, with Gesland body from the original Pannier depose. Value Points: rare larger size of the sought after doll with beautiful bisque and painting, choice sculpting of bisque limbs. $2500/3500

various serving dishes in white porcelain, along with green glass stemware and amber glassware, knives, forks and spoons for six, napkin rings for six, two spiral glass vases with flowers, and even tiny salt and pepper shakers in the shape of chicken and rooster. The pieces are fixed upon paper doilies with rose silk ribbons. Germany, circa 1910, an extensive and wonderfully-preserved set. $500/800

182. German Wooden Glass and Porcelain Shop with Unusual Curio Cabinet

25" (64 cm.) l. x 14"h. x 14"d. A wooden store with angled sides to give extra dimension to the store has ribbed columns with arched pediment at each side front, and an elaborate arrangement of shelving, cabinets, counter, and mirror, all of which are attached to the store walls and across the front opening. The store is painted original ochre with blue and red pencil-stripe trim, gilt painting on the mirror glass, and architectural details including clock, fret-work and shaped window frames on cabinet. There are original floor and wall papers, and an ormolu and glass chandelier suspends above. The store is lavishly furnished with a collection of miniature glass ware including rare faux-oil lamps, vases, pitchers and glasses, as well as porcelain statuary, tea set, and a collection of white bisque animal figures. A beautiful shop with Art Nouveau stylized features and unusual designs. Excellent condition except wall paper very worn. Germany, circa 1890. $2500/3500

181. German Miniature Porcelain and Glass Dinner Service for Six in Original Box

16" (41 cm.) x 9" box. 1 ½" glasses. A card stock box opens to reveal an extensive miniature dinner service for six, still tied into the original box, comprising plates, egg cups, rare fish mold, dessert plates, and

183. German Tin Fruit Stand with Awning by Bing with Crates of Fruits
9" (23 cm.) The tin outdoor stand with rope-shaped support poles and two shelves, has double-sided canvas action. Arranged on the tin shelves are wooden crates of paper mache fruits and vegetables including carrots, cucumbers, turnips and more, as well as a wooden crate of oranges with original label, an empty wooden crate with original paper label "Baby Apples" with image of baby, and a two bin wooden stand with grapes and asparagus. One box is stamped "G.B. 380", presumably Gebruder Bing. Structurally excellent, paint worn on tin stand. Germany, Gebruder Bing, circa 1890, very rare and delightful. $900/1300

184. Rare German Miniature Foods from the Fish Market
3 ½" (9 cm.) barrel. Including a wooden barrel with original "Sardines" label and having two sardines on the lid, two wooden crates labeled "Sardines" and filled with the little fish, two wooden buckets with chipped ice (one with fish), and two large paper mache trout. Excellent condition. Germany, circa 1890, rare. $300/500

185. German Wooden Butcher Shop with Rare Meats
15" (38 cm.) h. x 25"l. x 15"d. A wooden-framed two-room butcher shop has original cream and green painted facade and exterior walls, single multi-paned side window, originally painted interior walls with a ceiling border of pigs, and original paper flooring. The shop is fitted with attached shelving on three walls supporting metal racks with meat hooks. There are three additional cabinets and a front counter and chair. The shelves are laden with tinned foods and stoneware jars of labeled foods, and suspended from the racks are a vast number of cuts of meat, each of paper mache with painted and waxed finish. There are scales, cash register, slicers, and other tools, and a bisque woman and man with moustache stand in attendance. The waxed meats are extremely rare. Shop is in fair/good condition, unrestored. The contents are excellent. Germany, circa 1900. $2500/3500

186. Large German Wooden Two Story Furnished House with Painted Roof and Columns

40"l. (102 cm.) x 32" w. x 14" d. A wooden two-story stackable house has architectural columns at each side with painted blue and red decorations on cream background, painted red roof with defined shingles, painted blue side walls and two gables with opening windows. There are four rooms in the house, the bottom rooms with wide windows, and the upper rooms with set-back rooms (sunroom in the parlor, and bathroom in the bedroom). Each of the rooms has original floor and wall paper with beautiful tiny-scaled patterns, and the opening room door on the second floor is etched glass with a painted design of a rose. The house is well-furnished in classic over-crowded Victorian fashion and among its rare furnishings are a velvet-upholstered parlor set and an embossed maple dining set with extension dining table, sideboard, piano and more. Rare accessories include a goblet set in pewter holder, pewter cigar cutter, bear rug. Walterhausen wooden hanging clock, tin stove, and more. Fixtures hang in each room, and the house is peopled by five German bisque dollhouse people, while an upstairs maid shakes out sheets from the gable window. Excellent condition overall. Germany, circa 1890. $4000/6500

187. German Wooden Gazebo with Furnishings and Birdcage
11" (28 cm.) l. x 11"h. x 9"d. The wooden framed gazebo with attached window boxes on three sides and original floor, is furnished with painted white garden table and four chairs, and accented with soft metal bird cage and a set of lemonade glasses. Very good condition. Germany, circa 1900. $400/600

188. Fine Woven Dollhouse Sun Room Furnishings and Painted Tin Swing
5" (13 cm.) l. settee. Of finely-woven wicker in tiny appropriate scale, the set comprises settee, two arm chairs, two side chairs and pedestal table, in pristine condition. Along with a painted tin swing with original paint-grain finish to simulate wood, very good condition with few minor flakes. Germany, early-20th century. $300/500

189. German Miniature Bisque Dolls with Flowers
4" (10 cm.) and 3". Including bisque shoulderhead doll with blonde sculpted hair and painted hair bow, painted facial features, muslin body, bisque lower limbs, factory-original costume; along with all-bisque boy with blonde sculpted hair and painted features, factory original costume. The dolls are standing with a collection of miniature flowers and flower containers, including two painted tin jardinieres attributed to Maerklin, a painted tin early jardiniere with spiral twist legs, and a trellis with attached window box and flowers. Excellent condition, some paint flaking on one jardiniere. Germany, circa 1890. $300/500

190. German Wooden Garden Gazebo and Furnishings, with All-Bisque Doll
4" (10 cm.) doll. 7" gazebo. A wooden-framed gazebo with two benches and

original cotton awning is decorated with a garland of flowers. Along with matching bench, chair and table, and with additional flowers, paper mache gnome, tin watering can and rare aquarium. Included is an early all-bisque doll with swivel head, painted features, blonde mohair wig, peg-jointed limbs, painted yellow ankle boots, and wearing her original factory costume, marked 189. Excellent condition. Germany, circa 1900. $400/600

191. Collection of Seven French Doll-Sized Baskets

4" (10 cm.) -6". The woven baskets include double-sided market baskets, oval sewing baskets with lids and handles, wicker hamper containing porcelain miniature dishes (few flakes on dishes), and two additional baskets. Very good to excellent condition. French, circa 1890. $400/600

192. German Tin Dollhouse Furnishings

7" (18 cm.) cupboard. Comprising a tin kitchen cupboard and two chairs with lithographed finish to simulate wooden grain; and three-piece settee and two chairs in original painted green finish. Very good/excellent condition. Germany, circa 1885. $200/400

193. English Child's Soft-paste "Yellow Chick" Tea Set

4" (10 cm.) h. teapot. The creamy soft paste tea set has red pencil-stripe edging, and is decorated with amusing transfer designs of baby yellow chicks fighting over an earthworm, comprising lidded teapot, creamer, sugar bowl, three cups and saucers, three plates, marked "Made in England". Excellent condition. $200/400

194. German Child's Pottery Tea Service with Kitten Theme

3" (8 cm.) h. teapot. Of ceramic or pottery, with brilliant mustard yellow color, the tea set features amusing figural designs of a kitten, for example, the teapot being the body of the kitten with her left ear as a spout and her tail as a handle. The service comprises lidded teapot, creamer, lidded sugar, and six cups and saucer. Excellent overall with some roughness around cup rims. Germany, circa 1930. $200/400

195. Japan Ceramic Miniature Bunny Tea Set

3" (8 cm.) An amusing bunny figural tea set features a dressed bunny in green jacket and yellow breeches, the bunny body forming the pot with one arm as handle and one arm as spout, the set comprising lidded teapot, lidded sugar, creamer, and two cups and saucers. Marked Made in Japan. Excellent condition. Circa 1925. $100/200

196. French Bisque Character, 237, by SFBJ with Jewel-Like Eyes and Original Costume

14" (36 cm.) Solid domed bisque socket head, painted brown boyish hair, blue glass eyes with deep jewel-like effect, painted lashes and one-stroke brows, slightly-parted lips with row of porcelain teeth, French composition and wooden body jointed at shoulders and hips. Condition: bisque excellent, body original although paint flakes on limbs. Marks: 237 0. Comments: SFBJ, circa 1912. Value Points: fine quality of bisque enhanced by rich eyes, wearing original ivory silk faille sailor costume, cap, leather shoes. $1100/1500

197. Doll's Soft-Paste Jardiniere with Swan Designs

7" (18 cm.) The soft-paste one-piece jardiniere in classic design featuring double-handled urn shape on pedestal, is decorated with shaded blue-to-yellow coloring surrounding transfer images of swans. Excellent condition, rare to find and a wonderful doll accessory. Also included is a paper mache fur-covered seated cat with green glass eyes. Circa 1910. $300/500

197.1. German Wooden Doll Furniture by Moritz Gottschalk

9" (23 cm.) h. chair. Wooden porch furniture in the 1920s style includes a table and five chairs, each with original turquoise and cream paint. Excellent condition, virtually unplayed with. Germany, Moritz Gottschalk, circa 1920. $300/500

198. German Wooden Bakery and Grocery Store with Original Porcelain Labels

24" (61 cm.) l. x 15"h. x 16"d. The wooden store has a built-in cabinet against the back wall with 12 spice and condiment drawers centering a center display cabinet with mirrored front; there is built-in shelving on both sides that attaches to the front decorative columns and to the attached front counters. The store has original creamy-white painted finish with gold accents, and the drawers have porcelain labels and knobs. There is a matching free-standing counter. The store is well-laden with plates of wonderful pastries and other baked goods, and there are various tins, canisters and other containers, a paper roll with string holder, and other accessories.

A bisque head lady is standing behind the counter. Excellent condition. Germany, the store is attributed to Theodore Heymnann, circa 1925. $2500/3500

199. German Bisque Child Doll with Grocery Store and Contents

20" (51 cm.) cabinet. 19" doll. A bisque head doll with brown glass sleep eyes, painted features, open mouth, four porcelain teeth, brunette mohair wig, composition and wooden ball-jointed body, antique costume and apron, appears to be shopping from a white wooden store cabinet with painted brown spice drawers having tin spice labels. The store has a tin cash register, tin scale with brass trays, lamp, numerous food stuffs including glass bottles in metal tray, various tins, bottles, paper contains, a woven shopping basket filled with foods, and a supply of miniature cardboard boxed foods in their original factory box. Very good condition. Germany, doll is by Heinrich Handwerck. Circa 1900. $1200/1700

199.1. Tiny German Wooden Well-Filled Bakery

17" (43 cm.) l. x 9"h. x 8"d. The charming tiny bake shop has original cream-painted facade with blue trim and having two display windows, blue painted floor and exterior wall, and original interior wall and floor lithographed-paper covers. There is built-in shelving on the back wall with mirrored display niche, free-standing counter, and small hanging wall shelf. The shelves are filled with gesso or paper mache baked goods of all types, two sugar loafs, wooden boxes, and a rare tin display rack (probably Maerklin) with glass lidded jars. A glass lamp is suspended, and there are two people in the shop. Good condition. Germany, circa 1900. $700/1000

200. Rare German Painted Tin Bar by Maerklin
8" (20 cm.) The tinplate miniature bar with bottle shelves at the back wall having fretwork railing, attached semi-circular bar, and surmounting curved black-outlined red tin "Bar" sign, in original painted turquoise and tan. Along with bisque dollhouse man in original suit, and with selection of miniature glass liquer bottles. Good condition, original finish with some paint wear. Germany, Maerklin, circa 1910. $800/1000

201. Two German Tin Toy Automobiles
12" (30 cm.) and 8". Each is of tin with original painted or lithographed finish, including open-top car with driver, carriage lamps, running boards, and having mechanical clockwork with key (key missing); and maroon car with tin chauffeur, carriage lamps, headlights, spare tire, running board, and mechanical clockwork with attached key. Original finish on each with some minor wear. Germany, circa 1900. $400/600

202. German Wooden Art Deco Doll House Furnishings
3 ¾" (9 cm.) h. table. Wooden dining set of light oak features a table with pull-out leaves, four chairs with slip-in seats, and a buffet with curved front cabinets centering four drawers. Along with a slightly-smaller set of over-stuffed leather club chairs and matching sofa, and with desk lamp. Excellent condition, rare to find highly-stylized furnishings of fine quality. Germany, circa 1930. $400/600

203. Two German Bisque Dollhouse Men
6" (15 cm.) Each with bisque shoulder head, sculpted hair, painted facial features, muslin body, bisque lower limbs, including man with top hat, brown moustache, formal suit; and man with brown hair and curled tip moustache, black painted boots, and checkered wool driving costume. Excellent condition. Germany, circa 1910, rare features including top hat and moustaches $400/600

204. Pair, German Bisque Dolls by Kuhnlenz as Bride and Groom

16" (41 cm.) Each has bisque shoulder head, glass sleep eyes (he with brown eyes, she with blue eyes), painted lashes and brows, open mouth, four porcelain teeth, mohair wig, kid body with gusset-jointing at hips, knees and elbows, bisque lower arms. Condition: generally excellent. Marks: 309.5. Comments: Gebruder Kuhnlenz, circa 1890. Value Points: the dolls are wearing their original silk and woolen wedding costumes of bride and groom. $600/1000

205. French Candy Container as a Doll-Sized Bookcase

7" (18 cm.) A wooden-framed bookcase with natural finish has six bound sets of faux-books with gold-lettered trim and numbering; the books are actually lace-paper-edged boxes that once served for candy presentation from a luxury Parisian candy store. Excellent condition. French, circa 1880, rare and delightful candy container, designed for later use in doll play. $500/800

206. Rare Early French Candy Container as Clock Tower

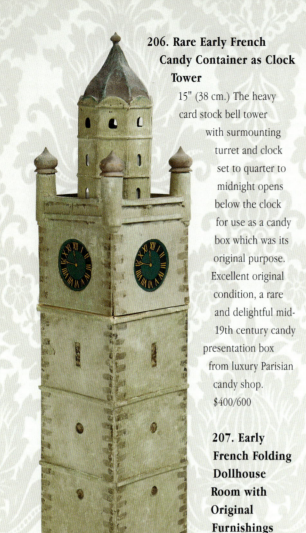

15" (38 cm.) The heavy card stock bell tower with surmounting turret and clock set to quarter to midnight opens below the clock for use as a candy box which was its original purpose. Excellent original condition, a rare and delightful mid-19th century candy presentation box from luxury Parisian candy shop. $400/600

207. Early French Folding Dollhouse Room with Original Furnishings

8" (20 cm.) h. room. 6"h. canopy. A five-panel folding room of heavy stock has two glass windows, original elaborate wall papers with gilt edging, original gilt paper valances and curtains with gilt-star appliques, four original engravings glued to walls with embossed gilt paper "frames". Along with original furnishings of natural wood with gilt paper edging, including sleigh bed with canopy, pedestal table, five chairs, fernery, and toilette table with mirror. The set is presented in its original box whose blue paper lining serves as the doll room floor. Excellent condition. French, circa 1875. $2000/2500

208. Early French Toy Games and Theatre with Pedestal Table

6" (15 cm.) h. table. A cherry and walnut marquetry pedestal table displays a walnut-framed theatre base with five scenes arranged dimensionally, along with a Loto game in original box, set of dominoes in original walnut sliding-lid box, tiny red dice in original box, and a walnut game box for checkers or backgammon. Very good condition, some paper loss on theatre, game sets may not be complete. French, circa 1875, perfect for display with poupées 17"-21". $400/600

209. Set of German Wooden Furnishings and All-Bisque Doll

7" (18 cm.) cabinet. A walnut desk with fretwork carving and blue paper lined interior is featured along with a matching settee and two chairs. Included is a 4" all-bisque doll with swivel head, brown glass eyes, open mouth, brunette mohair wig, peg-jointed bisque arms and legs with painted yellow stockings, and black two-strap shoes, antique costume. Excellent condition. Germany, circa 1890. $300/500

210. Fine Early Wooden Sleigh of Northern Netherlands with Oil-Painted Scenes

13" (33 cm.) The carved wooden sleigh is elaborately-shaped with scalloped-edging of carriage-body sides, curved rails that arch upward to support a plinth upon which is perched a carved wooden gilt lion. There is a wooden board at the back with studded brass plates, and a metal rod that supports the velvet-covered driver's seat. The passenger seat is also velvet-covered and both seats have metallic gilt fringe. The sleigh is accented with gilt striping, and there is a Holland painting on either side of the body, depicting a windmill and a ship sailing up a canal; two original wooden shafts for attachment to horse are included (not shown). $1200/1800

211. French Bisque Poupée by Jumeau with Salon Dog

15" (38 cm.) Bisque swivel head on kid-edged bisque shoulder plate, large blue glass enamel inset eyes, dark eyeliner, painted lashes and feathered brows, accented nostrils, closed mouth with outlined lips, pierced ears, blonde mohair wig over cork pate, French kid gusset-jointed body, stitched and separated fingers, wearing pretty antique gown, fur stole, undergarments, bonnet, nice leather boots. Condition: generally excellent, body somewhat weak at joints. Marks: 2 (head and shoulders) Jumeau Medaille d'Or Paris (body). Comments: Emile Jumeau, circa 1878. Value Points: very beautiful face with entrancing large eyes, original costume, included is French paper mache salon dog with white fur cover, amber glass eyes. $2000/3000

212. Grand French Crystal Chandelier

11" (28 cm.) l. including drops. The fine lead crystal chandelier is an elaborate confection of crystal beads, garlands, prismatic balls, and prismatic tears drops on metal and wire frame. Excellent condition. French, circa 1875, an especially fine and luxurious chandelier. $1500/2500

213. French Crystal Garland Chandelier

7" (18 cm.) A metal-framed chandelier is decorated with vertically-arranged garlands of prismatic crystal balls. Excellent condition. French, circa 1875. $500/700

214. Petite German Crystal and Opaline Bead Chandelier

3" (8 cm.) With brass cap and border, the chandelier is composed of garlands of clear crystal and opaline beads and rods. Excellent condition. Germany, circa 1890. $300/500

215. French Luxury Chandelier with Garlands and Tiered Drops

8" (20 cm.) Accented by beaded brass rims, the chandelier has graduated-size prismatic crystal beads above four tiers of crystal drops that are arranged around a metal orb-shaped frame. French, circa 1870, of very fine and luxury quality. Excellent condition. $1200/1700

216. French Crystal Chandelier with Elaborate Detail

11" (28 cm.) including tear drops. The wire-framed chandelier is lavishly-draped with crystal prismatic beads that drape from square "diamonds" to a border of square and round crystals, and there are additional tear drops and little wreaths of crystals. Excellent condition. French, circa 1875. $800/1200

217. French Fashion Engravings from Le Moniteur de la Mode
14" (36 cm.) x 10". Four fashion engravings depict fashionable ladies and girls from the 1880/1890 era, with original paper edging and glass, three from Le Moniteur de la Mode and one from Revue de La Mode, along with three smaller engravings also under glass. Good condition, some light spotting. $200/400

218. French Bisque Poupée with Cobalt Blue Eyes, Signed B.S.
16" (41 cm.) Bisque shoulder head with plump facial modeling, brilliant cobalt blue glass enamel eyes, dark eyeliner, delicately-feathered lashes and brows, accented nostrils, closed mouth with accented lips, un-pierced ears, light brown mohair wig over cork pate, French kid poupée body with shapely torso, gusset-jointing at hips, knees and elbows, stitched and separated fingers, wearing beautiful antique silk costume, undergarments, leather shoes. Condition: generally excellent. Marks: B.4 S. Comments: attributed to Blampoix, circa 1865. Value Points: pleasing expression with contrasting pale cobalt blue eyes, very sturdy body. $1200/1800

219. German Gilt Metal Five-Arm Chandelier
8" (20 cm.) A cast metal chandelier has center rod with five fancily-scrolled arms supporting gilt metal orbs with original milk glass shades. Excellent condition. Germany, circa 1900. $300/500

220. Fine French Inlay Toilette Table for Poupée
10" (25 cm.) closed. 15" with mirror. Of fine mahogany with burled inlay veneers, the elegant toilette table has three hinged compartments on the table top that hinge open, the center with a mirror, and the other two for storage, each with original patterned silk lining. Below the center compartment is a pull-out shelf, and there are two small drawers. French, circa 1875, the luxurious quality of craftsmanship and fine woods indicate its original presentation in Parisian store such as Maison Giroux. $900/1300

221. Two French Miniature Accessories for Poupées
6" (15 cm.) vase. Including a turquoise blue vase with multi-colored beaded floral design and having unusual slender neck, attached to original cast brass three-legged base. Along with a wooden box with inlay lattice design on the lid, hinged lid, and impressed name "Fountainebleu". Excellent condition. French, circa 1880, perfectly sized for display with 16"-18" poupée or small bébés. $300/500

222. French Doll's Chair from the Napoleon III Era with Original Upholstery
10" (25 cm.) The wood-framed chair is entirely-upholstered excepting the four feet hidden behind the fringed trim, with thick firmly-stuffed padding and tapestry cover, trimmed with thick braided fringe and cording. Excellent condition. French, Napoleon III era. $400/600

223. French Paper Mache Salon Dog
7" (18 cm.) A firm-sided standing dog with lavish white fur coat, shaved face and lower legs, amber glass eyes, carved open mouth. Excellent condition. French, circa 1890. $300/500

224. French Bisque Poupée by Gaultier in Antique Costume

16" (41 cm.) Bisque swivel head on kid-edged bisque shoulder plate, pale blue glass enamel inset eyes, delicately-painted lashes and brows, accented nostrils, closed mouth with outlined lips, pierced ears, brunette mohair wig over cork pate, French kid gusset-jointed body with stitched and separated fingers. Condition: generally excellent. Marks: 3 (head and shoulders). Comments: Gaultier, circa 1875. Value Points: beautiful bisque and painting, fine sturdy body, wearing beautiful antique brown silk gown with blue trim undergarments, silk bonnet, leather ankle boots, and having original wig with original paper label "3" indicating matched size to head. $2000/2800

225. French Wooden Toy Piano with Blue Wild Flower Decorations

11" (28 cm.) x 11". The wooden upright piano is painted original creamy white with painted decorations of dainty blue wild flowers and leaves, and with blue edged borders and trim, cast brass handles at the side, with 12 working keys (one note not sounding), and hinged keyboard cover. Along with a pair of porcelain statuary depicting a boy and girl at play with teddy bears, and a gilded metal urn of flowers. French, circa 1890. $400/600

226. Tiny Dollhouse Room with Original Furnishings

11" (28 cm.) l. x 4"h. x 8"d. The heavy-stock framed room has gilt paper edging and original floor paper to simulate parquet and original wallpaper with painted ribbon picture hangings, various small prints, and has original furnishings of aqua tufted sateen with gilt wood frames, metal fireplace, with little girl and toys. Excellent condition. Circa 1890. Excellent condition. $300/400

227. Set of Three Antique Miniature Impressionist Oil Paintings on Board

6" (15 cm.) largest. The set of three impressionist oil paintings on board depict sea scenes with intriguing day and night moon light reflections, stormy sky and blue sky, framed to match. Unsigned. Excellent condition, and of fine artistry. Late-19th century. $400/600

228. 19th Century Wooden Play Harp for Poupée

14" (36 cm.) The floor-standing wooden harp has original burgundy red finish enhanced by gilt accents on the gesso-sculpted designs. Very good condition, original painted finish with some flakes. Mid-19th century. $300/500

229. Petite French Bisque Poupée, Size 0, in Original Muslin Gown

11" (28 cm.) Bisque shoulder head doll has brilliant cobalt blue glass enamel eyes, painted lashes and brows, accented nostrils, closed mouth with hint of smile, brunette mohair wig over cork pate, French kid gusset-jointed body with stitched and separated fingers. Condition: generally excellent. Marks: 0. Comments: Barrois, circa 1865. Value Points: desirable size 0, the little girl wears her original simple stiffened muslin gown with black muslin insets and lace trim, undergarments, shoes. $1100/1500

230. Rare Grand German Room from the Biedermeier Era with Chinoiserie Papers

49" (124 cm.) l. x 19"h. x 20"d. The large two-room wooden doll house has papered exterior to simulate marble, four large windows, double opening doors between the rooms, and original interior floor paper to simulate parquet, and wall paper in the Chinoiserie style with black paper borders, and gilt edging. The rooms have antique maroon silk and velvet curtains and valances with gold braid and pom-poms. and the furnishings include crystal chandelier, rare velvet-upholstered oak furnishings, maroon velvet upholstered furnishings, marble top pieces and tall chests, Accessories include grand ormolu hall mirror, well-laden tables of soft pewter, salon dog, wonderful prints and wall hangings, needlework carpets, and more. The house is attended by three gentlemen (two with moustache) and a lady. Good condition, with some separation, one trim missing on double door, paper is original albeit worn. Germany, circa 1875, rare early room in grand size. $3500/4500

231. French Maple Wood Doll's Salon Set

11" (28 cm.) h. The three-piece set of maple wood with natural finish and bamboo-shaped styling has aqua silk tufted upholstery, comprising settee and two matching chairs. Structurally excellent, upholstery is original albeit frail. French, circa 1880. $700/1000

232. Beautiful French Bisque Portrait Doll by Jumeau with Exquisite Costume and Original Paper Label

16" (41 cm.) Pressed bisque socket head, almond-shaped blue glass enamel inset eyes with spiral-threading, dark eyeliner, mauve-blushed eye shadow, painted lashes and brows, accented nostrils, closed mouth with accent line between the lips, pierced ears, blonde mohair wig over cork pate, French wooden bébé body with jointing at shoulders, elbows, hips and knees. Condition: bisque and body excellent albeit not original to each other. Marks: 7 (head) A La Mignonette Poupées et Bébés Costumes et Trousseaux Mon Guigue 7 rue Notre Dame de Lorette (original paper label on body). Comments: portrait bisque head by Jumeau, circa 1875, body is probably by Bru of which the costume appears to be original, and probably offered in the A La Mignonette shop, circa 1880s.

Value Points: exquisite face and painting, gorgeous albeit frail costume of aqua silk with extended train, aqua wool cap, aqua stockings and black leather shoes stamped E. Jumeau Med d'Or Paris. $3000/4000

233. French Tin Miniature Sleigh with Painted Cherub Decorations

7" (18 cm.) The winter sleigh with beautifully-curved sides is resting upon a cast brass sleigh base with ornate crest; the tin is painted bronze-gold with scenes of flowers, winged cherubs on clouds, and garland borders, and the interior is lined with plum velvet, from a series of similarly-decorated miniature furniture whose original purpose was as jewelry or watch display, yet perfectly-scaled for display with small dolls. Very good condition, one side has paint loss. French, circa 1880, the sleigh being a rare variation from the series. $400/600

234. French Toilette Set in Original Presentation Box

9" (23 cm.) x 6" box. The light-wood box with decorative paper covers hinges open to reveal an elaborately-fitted interior having lace-border around a mirror on inside lid trimmed with rose silk ribbons; with shelved base edged with gold paper borders, and containing porcelain wash bowl and pitcher with floral designs, along with four matching jars or boxes, and with towels, powder puffs, and more. Excellent condition, rim flake on pitcher. French, circa 1890. $400/600

235. 19th Century Miniature Buffet with Porcelain Tête-à-Tête

10" (25 cm.) h. buffet. 3" tray. A mahogany buffet with mirrored back, two drawers and two lower cabinets, is set with a porcelain tea set, with white background decorated with green pencil-stripe garlands, gold edging and colorful flowers, comprising scalloped-edge tray, lidded teapot and sugar, creamer, and two cups and saucers. Excellent condition. Circa 1900. $300/500

236. Petite French Bisque Poupée, Size 3/0

10" (25 cm.) Bisque swivel head on kid-edged shoulder plate, blue glass eyes, painted lashes, feathered brows, accented nostrils, closed mouth with center accent line, pierced ears, blonde mohair wig over cork pate, French kid poupée body with shapely torso and legs, mitten hands, nicely costumed in white muslin gown, undergarments, tiny black kidskin shoes, bonnet. Condition: generally exellent. Marks: 3/0. Comments: French, circa 1875. Value Points: wonderful petite size is rare to find. $1100/1400

237. German Porcelain Tea Service in Unusual Square-Shape

4" (10 cm.) h. pot. Of fine porcelain with embossed details, white background with gold edging and transfer-designs of rose buds, the service is in an unusual diagonally-arranged square shape with scroll handles, and includes lidded teapot, lidded sugar, creamer and four cups and saucers. Excellent condition, finial imperceptively reglued on sugar lid. Germany, circa 1890. $300/500

matching bucket, and various combs and brushes, as well as a fitted store box of accessories including powder puff and soap. Excellent condition. French, circa 1900. $600/900

240. French Porcelain Wash Bowl and Pitcher, with Statuary Jar

4" (10 cm.) The white porcelain wash bowl and pitcher are decorated with pink borders and black stenciled designs and has blue gargoyle-shaped handle, along with a porcelain statue of aristocratic man, which opens at his ankles to reveal a trinket box. Excellent condition. French, circa 1885. $300/4500

238. French Bisque Bébé Dep in Original Chemise

15" (38 cm.) Bisque socket head, dark blue glass inset eyes, painted lashes, brush-stroked brows, accented nostrils and eye corners, closed mouth, pierced ears, blonde mohair wig, French composition and wooden fully-jointed body. Condition: generally excellent. Marks: Dep 6. Comments: circa 1900. Value Points: the pretty bébé has rarer closed mouth, original body and body finish, and wears her original muslin dress with lace trim. $800/1100

239. French Wooden Toilette Table with Faience Wash Set

13" (33 cm.) The wooden toilette stand has oval-shaped table top having a cut-out insert for placement of wash bowl, and knobs for placement of barrel-shaped water container that swings back and forth to empty water into the bowl. The table has fine cotton covers, original creamy softpaste bowl and pitcher with

cover with blue fringe; wooden handled parasol with striped silk cover; and celluloid-handled parasol with lace cover. Good to excellent condition. Also included is a brass holder for use as parasol cover. Suitable for display with bébés 22"-25". French, late-19th century. $600/900

241. Petite French Doll Costume in Early Box

6" (15 cm.) h. costume. For doll about 10". Comprising a white pique jacket with faux-double-breasted design, with white cotton skirt having soutache trim around the hem. The costume is preserved in an early box with lithograph on front lid. Excellent condition albeit dusty. French, circa 1880. $200/400

242. Vintage Needlepoint Carpet with Toy and Doll Theme

23" (58 cm.) x 17". The needlework tapestry or carpet with muslin lining, has royal blue background and depicts a wonderful collection of antique dolls and toys including pull toy animals, drums, dolls, rocking horses and more. Excellent condition. Late-19th century. $300/500

243. Three French Bébé Parasols

11" (28 cm.) l. parasols. Including wooden handled parasol with brass figural dog's head grip and black silk

244. French Porcelain Tea Service in Original Box

5" (13 cm.) teapot. 15" x 11" box. A red card-stock box with yellow edging has a blue paper interior that is fitted to accommodate the porcelain tea set that it encloses, the set of white porcelain with gold borders and dainty decorations of delicate gold chain garlands, roses, and blue stars, comprising lidded teapot, lidded sugar, creamer, and six cups and saucers. Excellent condition. French, circa 1885. $300/500

245. Miniature Portrait in Oval Frame

3 ½" (9 cm.) The gouache painting on heavy paper depicts an elegant woman in soft pastel colors, signed Duval, and presented in fine antique frame with garland ribbon trim. The back papers are ink-inscribed Marie de la Fontaine. Age uncertain. $200/300

246. Wonderful German Dollhouse Kitchen with Farmyard Scene Wallpaper

31" (79 cm.) . x 16" x 17". The large one-room wooden kitchen is brightly-papered with sea-blue and pale yellow checkered wall-paper, that is accented with wide floor and ceiling borders depicting garden and farmyard scenes including a kneeling gnome offering flowers to a bunny, and with contrasting lattice-patterned floor papers. The wooden frame has natural finish, and the exterior has faux-brick paper cover. There is a large window at the back with original cornice and the kitchen has its original furnishings including a long work counter with windowed base, tall narrow cupboard, hanging plate rack, buffet, hanging spice rack, bench, table with drawer and two chairs, each with original cream paint accented with blue stripes. The tin stove with chrome surface and original lidded pots and stove pipe stands at the back, and the kitchen contains a grand assortment of rare accessories including tin coffee grinder, wire pie cover, rare wooden-handled iron, copper tea pot, tin wall sink, stenciled tin lunch bucket, wooden towel rack with porcelain labels, wooden laundry tub with wringer, glass cake cover, and numerous porcelain dishes and spice jars. A bisque doll with original house maid's costume stands at the back. Germany, circa 1910. Excellent condition. $2200/3500

247. German Wooden Toy Kitchen with Basket of Chickens
25" (64 cm.) l. x 14"h. x 4"d. The wooden framed one-room kitchen has five-sided walls with one multi-paned window in the Gottschalk construction style, white painted frame and exterior, original wall and floor papers, the wall paper simulating Dutch tiles with ceiling border of a Dutch-costumed girl giving her doll yarn to wind. The kitchen is furnished with matching cupboard, sideboard, work table and two chairs having light cream finish to simulate pine wood, There is a wire-screen door pie safe at the back, a hanging wooden rack with kitchen utensils and a tin stove with brass doors and original pots and chimney. Accessories include a wood-framed tin scale, meat grinders, clock, tin wall sink, wooden hanging towel rack with porcelain labels, wire onion rack, tin trash bucket "Abfalle" with lid, various porcelain jars and dishes including labeled sardine container, a basket of chickens whose heads are peeking out of the basket they are resting in, and a wooden egg rack with the eggs the chickens have aid. Contents excellent, room has wear at caps of corner posts and floor frame, wonderful original wall paper with some paper rubs. Germany, probably Gottschalk, circa 1920. $1500/2500

248. German Bisque Doll by Kammer and Reinhardt with Kitchen Cabinet and Dishes

32" (81 cm.) h. cabinet. 27" doll. A bisque head doll with blue glass sleep eyes, painted features, open mouth, four porcelain teeth, blonde mohair wig, composition and wooden ball-jointed body, antique costume and apron, is standing alongside a wooden kitchen cabinet with drawers, shelves and cupboards, that is filled with a lavish white porcelain child's dinnerware service by Villeroy and Boch, the set with impressed ribbed pattern and blue designs, and comprising more than 35 pieces including both serving dishes and place settings, along with wrapped table cloths. The doll is marked K*R. Excellent condition. Germany, doll by Kammer and Reinhardt, dishes by Villeroy and Boch, circa 1910. $900/1100

249. Grand German Wooden Child's Play Kitchen on Original Table

30" (76 cm.) h. without table. 55" with table. 45" length. 24" d. A large one-room kitchen with two back windows has original worn frame paint and exterior papers (split on back wall between windows), and original floor paper to simulate tiles, and half-wall paper with blue Delft tile design. A large Maerklin stove with brass oven doors and original nickel kitchen pots stands in the middle of the room, and there are two large white cupboards (one with

painted glass lower panels), a smaller wooden table and chairs designed for the use of the doll's doll. The room is generously filled with rare kitchen accessories, including hanging shelf with pewter cups, blue and white Delft porcelain canisters, early stoneware pottery, collection of tin and earthenware pudding molds, enamel sieves, brass scale, coffee grinder, set of wooden decorated tubs, set of enamel cups, saucers and coffee pot, oil lamp, onion bag with wire frame and more. Standing in the kitchen is a German bisque doll marked 1902 3/0 with blue glass sleep eyes, brunette braided wig, and antique cotton pinafore costume. The kitchen rests upon its original table with center drawer and original paint-grained finish to simulate wood. Good condition, with play wear. Germany, circa 1890, the grand size of the kitchen suggests its original exhibition purpose or deluxe nature. $3000/4500

250. German Wooden Butcher Shop with Free-Standing Rack
20" (51 cm.) l. x 10"h. x 11"d. The wooden one-room butcher shop has frame and exterior of natural wood and pale green painted wood, and the interior has painted green upper walls above lithographed paper to simulate tiles; lithographed-paper "tiles" cover the floor. There is attached shelving on the back wall with chrome hanging racks for meat, free-standing counter, more chrome racks attached to the side walls, and a free-standing wooden rack with suspended poultry and fowl. The counter has a tin cash register, a rare wooden and metal slicer, and plates of meat, a large paper mache pig head designed as a sign is attached to the center back wall, and dozens of paper mache or gesso cuts of meat are suspended on metal hooks or arranged on plates, ready for sale. A bisque dollhouse lady stands behind the counter and a wooden sign "Fleisch und Wurstwaren" stands in its original tin base. Very good condition overall. Germany, circa 1900, a rare well-laden store with rare accessories such as meat slicer. $2000/3000

251. 19th Century Doll-Sized Kitchen Accessories
6" (15 cm.) square butcher block. A heavy wooden butcher block with knife slits, with assortment of toy sausages and meats; along with a set of graduated-size cast copper pots with brass handles, a wooden slicing board with attached cast iron rack and wooden-handled knife; various bone-handled cutlery, and two blue-decorated stoneware jugs, one with Frankfurt signature. Excellent condition. Germany/France, circa 1885. $1200/1500

252. German Bisque Doll with Grocery Store Cabinet and Foods 27" (69 cm.) h. x 24"h. x 8"d. 26" doll. A wooden store counter with original white painted finish with gold accents has porcelain labels and knobs on the bottom cupboard and spice drawers, with upper glass sided and shelved cabinet and slant-front accounts desk. The store is generously filled with rare tins and canisters, baskets of other victuals including Nurnberger Lebkucken. There is a brass iron scale with brass trays, a paper mache duck, a mohair black cat5, and other charming accessories, along with a bisque doll, model 390, by Armand Marseille with antique costume. Excellent condition. Germany, circa 1910. $1200/1800

253. Large German Wooden Dollhouse for the French Market, Probably Gottschalk

34" (86 cm.) The large two-story dollhouse has lithographed paper cover to simulate architectural details, over-hanging front porch roof with columns, opening door with classic Gottschalk silver handle, three glass windows at the front and two at each side, extended-height (removable) turret with blue steeple roof, and original base with marbled platform to simulate stone foundation. Access to the house interior is at either side, both sides hinging open to the four interior rooms with opening doors between and having fine original wall and floor papers. Good condition of exterior with some paper wear, interior excellent. Germany, probably Gottschalk, circa 1900, for the French market. $2000/3000

254. German Wooden Blue Roof Dollhouse with Steeple Turret
26" (66 cm.) Wooden two-story dollhouse has lithographed paper cover to simulate architectural details including door and windows, with hinged front that opens to two interior rooms. There is a wooden over-hanging front door roof, a wooden porch railing with gilt cardboard trim, and marbleized base. The painted blue roof has gabled section, and a removable turret with steeple roof and weathervane, chimney. Excellent condition. Germany, circa 1900. $1200/1800

255. German Wooden Blue Roof Dollhouse with Elevator by Moritz Gottschalk
20" (51 cm.) The two-story wooden dollhouse has painted blue roof and painted and lithographed exterior to simulate architectural details, with wooden porch or balcony with gilt paper railings on both floors, over-hanging porch roof on second floor, four glass front windows, two opening doors (one with original Gottschalk silver door knob), two interior rooms and two smaller foyer rooms with elevator that operates by turning knob at the side. Good/very good condition. Germany, Moritz Gottschalk, Germany, circa 1900. $2200/3200

256. German Wooden Cottage Dollhouse, Possibly Schonherr
17" (43 cm.) x 21" x 14"d. The one-room cottage dollhouse with hinged front, has working front door, glass windows at the front with painted shutters, wide front porch with grand columns and porch railing, original base with lithographed paper stonework, four-window roof gable, two chimneys. Good condition. Germany, possibly Albin Schonherr, circa 1920. $900/1500

- 123 -

257. French Bisque Poupée with Cobalt Blue Glass Eyes
13" (33 cm.) Bisque swivel head on kid-edged bisque shoulder plate, cobalt blue glass eyes, delicately-painted lashes and brows, accented nostrils and eye corners, closed mouth with center accent line, unpierced ears, brunette mohair wig over cork pate, kid poupée body with gusset-jointing at hips and knees, wearing antique white day ensemble, coronet, undergarments, leather shoes. Condition: generally excellent. Comments: French, circa 1860. Value Points: charming petite poupée whose brilliant eyes contrast with her very beautiful pale complexion, fine antique costume $1200/1700

258. Collection of Vintage Christmas Decorations and Wooden Cupboard
12" (30 cm.) The Christmas tree on original wooden base has silver glass balls and candle loops, along with a table centerpiece with wooden base supporting its original wreath, a box of miniature silver balls, and a floor standing corner cabinet base for display. Excellent condition. Late-19th century. $400/600

259. Cast Iron Parlor Stove for Doll Room
4" (10 cm.) Of heavy cast iron with elaborate detail of grill work and fender, and having original dark bronze-like finish. Excellent condition. 19th century. $200/400

262. Early Cast Brass Fireplace
6" (15 cm.) h. x 7"w. The heavy cast brass fireplace has richly-designed mantel and facade, and detail of grill and fender. Excellent condition. 19th century. $200/400

263. French Marquetry Pedestal Table with German All-Bisque Doll and Holiday Trees

15" (38 cm.) larger tree. 6"h. table. A fine pedestal table with elaborate marquetry table top of various woods, displays a small antique Christmas tree with candles and tiny glass balls, along with a larger holiday tree with silver ball garland, glass balls, candles and bent-wire star-shaped tree topper, on wooden base; and an all-bisque doll with glass inset eyes, jointed limbs, and unusual original costume. Excellent condition. Late-19th Century $900/1400

264. Petite French Bisque Poupée with Dainty Expression

12" (31 cm.) Bisque swivel head on kid-edged bisque shoulder plate, cobalt blue glass enamel eyes, dark eyeliner, painted lashes and brows, accented nostrils closed mouth with center accent line, pierced ears, blonde mohair wig over cork pate, French poupée kid body with gusset-jointing at hips, knees and elbows, wearing antique red cotton gown with black velvet trim, undergarments, ankle boots, woolen cape with silk fringe and cap. Condition: generally excellent. Comments: French, circa 1865. Value Points: very dear petite size with arresting blue eyes, pretty costume. $1200/1700

265. Collection of Vintage Christmas Ephemera
12" (30 cm.) tree. Including holiday tree on wooden base with glass balls and attached tiny red and green lights; large Santa boot with plush finish and wreath collar and filled with wooden Erzebirg toys; a smaller paper mache Santa boot with toys; paper mache snow man and St. Nicholas figures, set of six-sided miniature blocks with lithographed images in original box; and more. Excellent condition. Early-20th century. $600/900

266. Sonneberg Bisque Doll in the French Look-Alike Manner

11" (28 cm.) Solid domed bisque socket head, blue glass inset eyes, painted lashes and brows, accented nostrils, closed mouth with accented lips, pierced ears, brunette mohair wig, Sonneberg composition and wooden eight-loose-ball jointed body, wearing pretty antique costume. Condition: generally excellent. Marks: 3. Comments: Sonneberg, circa 1885, the doll closely resembles the early portrait bébés by Jumeau, whose market the Sonneberg maker was attempting to capture. Value Points: pretty child with endearing shy expression, original body and body finish. $800/1000

267. French Bisque Bébé Jumeau in Original Costume

18" (46 cm.) Bisque socket head, blue glass paperweight inset eyes, dark eyeliner, painted lashes and brows, accented nostrils and eye corners, open mouth, row of porcelain teeth, pierced ears, brunette mohair wig over cork pate, French composition and wooden fully-jointed body. Condition: generally excellent. Marks: 6 (head) Jumeau Diplome d'Honneur (paper label on body). Comments: Emile Jumeau, circa 1895. Value Points: the wide-eyed boy is wearing his original brown woolen suit with silk vest and brass buttons, straw hat, stockings, brown kidskin shoes signed Paris Bébé with bee symbol. $1700/2600

268. Two German Toy Horses

9" (23 cm.) platform length. Each is firm-constructed horse with glass eyes, and original factory leather harness and equipment, one on wooden platform with cast iron wheels and (worn) hide cover, and the other with brushed brown wool cover. Very good condition. Germany, late-19th century. $400/600

269. German Brown-Complexioned Bisque Child, 949, by Simon and Halbig

13" (33 cm.) Bisque socket head with brown complexion, brown glass set eyes, painted features, open mouth, four tiny porcelain teeth, pierced ears, black mohair wig, brown composition and wooden fully-jointed body with straight wrists, nicely costumed in antique school dress. Condition: generally excellent. Marks: 949 S&H. Comments: Simon and Halbig, circa 1890. Value Points: charming petite model of the hard to find early doll with rare brown complexion, original body and body finish. $800/1100

270. French Paper Mache Candy Container as Tabby Kitten

7" (18 cm.) The paper mache cat has painted grey/cream tabby finish with extended tail, green glass eyes and removable head for candy storage. Good condition with repair at tail. French, circa 1890. $200/400

271. German Wooden Grocery Store with Lithographed Tin Labels by August Hermann

30" (76 cm.) x 16"h. x 11"d. A wooden grocery store with natural wood finish on front and interior shelving has originally painted ochre exterior with red pencil striping. There are two hinged display windows at the front that swing open for easy play, and the entire back wall is fitted with drawers, shelving and display niches separated by fancy columns and arches. Each of 16 drawers has its original lithographed tin label with name. There is a free-standing matching counter, and the store is filled with various groceries, tins, canisters and supplies including a rare floor scale, lithographed tin cabinet, and paper roll. Excellent condition. Germany, attributed to August Hermann, circa 1890. $2500/3000

272. Rare German Wooden Fully-Furnished Miniature "Leder-Waren Handlung" Shop

32" (81 cm.) l. 16" h. x 13"d. The wooden framed shop with original painted cream finish trimmed with gold on the exterior facade, grey painted sides, and original wall and floor interior papers, has display windows at both sides with detailed architectural trim, and arched glass windows with original gold lettering "Leder-Waren Handlung" (leather ware shop). Built-in shelving, cabinets and display niches cover the back wall with a centering arch and railed balcony. The center display niche has shaped shelves. There is a free-standing matching counter. The shop is filled with a generous bounty of goods for sale, comprising both leather and faux-leather valises, trunks, bags, belts, gloves, purses and more. A parchment-paper lamp with glass beads is suspended above, and a bisque-head lady stands behind the counter. Very good condition, original finish is worn. Germany, circa 1900, the gold lettering indicates the shop was originally presented as a leather goods store, and is very rare. $3500/5500

273. Petite Early Wooden Dollhouse with Furnishings and Family

26" (66 cm.) h. x 20"l. x 12"d. A well-detailed house two-story house with both front and side windows, architectural details on the exterior enhanced by lithographed paper brick and green painted trim. The interior has four rooms, including living room with red velvet upholstered furnishings and Walterhausen marble top desk and cabinet; the kitchen has painted furnishings and tin stove; the upper salon has rare silk upholstered furnishings with fringed detail, fireplace, piano, cabinet and marble-top table; and the small nursery has swinging soft metal cradle, sewing table, fireplace, and chairs. Accessories include tiger head rug, silver service, books, candle holders, easel with print, parlor stove, and much more. Eight people live in the home. Good condition except the roof sides are very worn, interior wall and floor papers original. Germany, circa 1880, a wonderful size house with charming furnishings and people. $2000/3000

274. Set of German Cast Iron Gas Lamps

17" (43 cm.) Five standing lamp posts, each with one, two or three lamps, have cast iron posts with faux-wooden base and bronze-like posts and fixtures, with glass globes. Probably Maerklin. Very good, excellent condition. Early-20th century. $200/500

275. Mid-19th Century American Patented Mechanical Doll by Goodwin, with Dog

11" (28 cm.) A lady doll with pressed-cloth head in the manner of paper mache dolls has blonde sculpted hair with head band, painted earrings, painted facial features, original body with hidden mechanism, cast iron hands and feet, and pushing three-wheeled tin cart with cast iron spoked wheels. When wound, the doll should "walk", pushing the carriage. Condition: fair, unrestored, with craquelure on head, costume not original, original painted on cart albeit worn on cart bed. Marks: LCR 1868... (partial paper sticker on head). Comments: the doll by George Hawkins who patented the unique construction style in 1868, and with original use as the doll for the patented William Goodwin lady with cart toy. Included are cart objects, and the flannel-covered dog with amber glass eyes. $800/1300

276. German Paper Mache Doll with Enamel Eyes and Rare Stitched-On Gloves

22" (56 cm.) Paper mache shoulder head with sculpted black hair in long ringlet curls tucked behind her sculpted ears, black enamel eyes, painted lashes and brows, accented nostrils, closed mouth, muslin stitch-jointed body with stitched on and painted brown gloves, antique silk dress, undergarments, stockings, shoes. Condition: original finish is well-preserved except horizontal separation across the lower back shoulder plate. Comments: Germany, circa 1860. Value Points: very charming face, with rare glass eyes and ringlet curls, rare original body with sewn-on gloves. $300/500

277. German Carved Wooden Doll Head

5 ½" (14 cm.) Carved wooden shoulder head with deeply chip-carved short curly hair arranged in scalloped curls around her face, painted upper glancing eyes, lashes and brows, closed mouth with shaded lips. Very good/excellent original finish with light nose rub. Germany, circa 1860. $300/500

278. French Bisque Poupée and Her Miniature Dogs

13" (33 cm.) Bisque swivel head on kid-edged bisque shoulder plate, plump cheeks, cobalt blue glass enamel eyes, painted lashes, feathered brows, accented nostrils, closed mouth with accented lips, ears pierced into head, brunette mohair wig over cork pate, French kid poupée body with gusset-jointing, antique gown, undergarments, stockings, bonnet. Condition: generally excellent. Marks: 1. Comments: circa 1870. Value Points: pretty bright-eyed lady with dramatic eyes; included are two 3" miniature salon dogs in rare size. $1200/1800

279. French Chair and Stool for Poupée

10" (25 cm.) Of wood with original ebony black finish and gilt stenciled trim, the salon chair has nicely scalloped carving and decoration on the back rests, and spindled legs, with turquoise silk seat and braid trim, and with ebony-finished stool with matching upholstery. Excellent condition, upholstery a bit dusty. $300/500

280. Rare Early English Soft-Paste Partial Miniature Dinner Service by Thomas Dimmock

6" (15 cm.) largest platter. Of creamy soft-paste with black transfer designs, the service comprises small lidded tureen, sauce boat, oval bowl, three graduated size platters, two oval platters, six dinner plates, six dessert plates, and four soup bowls. Excellent condition albeit incomplete. English, attributed to Thomas Dimmock, circa 1850. $300/500

281. Two Miniature Services for Petite Dolls including Sevres Tea Set

3" (8 cm.) tray. Comprising a tiny porcelain service with painted and decorated yellow background centering a wreathed medallion and with exterior border of garland and gold edging, including tray, pot, sugar, creamer and two cups and saucers, marked Sevres in blue stamp, along with a blown glass wine service with amber glass stems comprising a tray, handled carafe, and six goblets. Excellent condition. Late-19th century. $300/500

281.1. Rare Tiny Fish-Bone Carved Tea Set

3 ½" (9 cm.) l. tray. An exquisitely-painted very tiny tea set is carved entirely of delicate fish bones, and comprises lidded teapot, creamer, sugar, bowl and six cups. Excellent condition. Mid-19th century. $200/400

282. French Bisque Poupée as Head Housekeeper by Gaultier

16" (41 cm.) Bisque swivel head on kid-edged bisque shoulder-plate, blue glass enamel inset eyes, delicately-painted lashes and brows, accented nostrils and eye corners, closed mouth with accented lips, pierced ears, blonde mohair wig over cork pate, French kid poupée body with shapely torso, gusset-jointed elbows, hips and knees, stitched and separated fingers. Condition; generally excellent. Marks: 2 (head and shoulders). Comments: Gaultier, circa 1875. Value Points: the lovely doll wears her original Head Housekeeper ensemble with black velvet jacket, taffeta skirt, undergarments, kidskin shoes, cap, and beautiful antique chatelaine and scissors. $2800/3600

283. English Doll-sized Fruitwood Buffet with Accessories

14" (36 cm.) l. x 14"h. x 6". Of very fine wood, the honey-brown finish and having burled walnut panels on cabinet doors, the buffet has arched crest, two silverware drawers, six lower drawers and two angled side cabinets, with unusual crystal pulls. Displayed on the buffet is a three-piece matched set of vases and urn with strawberry theme, along with a bisque casserole dish with figural duck as the lid. Excellent condition. Late-19th century. $500/800

284. English Wooden Doll House with Furnishings

31" (79 cm.) "h. x 21"w. x 10"d. A petite two-story wooden dollhouse with brown painted exterior having grey, blue, and cream trim has two brass cherubs decorating the roof line, with shutters and window plant ledges on the six exterior front windows, and an open front entry with porch. The interior has three rooms, each with built-in fireplace and chimney, including a large parlor and dining room on the first floor furnished with maple set having maroon velvet upholstery and white marble tops. The second floor has a bedroom with more maple furnishings and the third floor is a gentleman's study. Accessories including prints and engravings, clocks, hanging light fixtures, statues, dishes, globe, books, carved bone dice, bearskin rug, and more. The front facade removes for access to the rooms. Very good condition, the exterior is repainted, the interior has old wallpapers and wooden floors. English, late-19th century. $1100/1500

285. Small German Two-Room Wooden Dollhouse with Furnishings

29" (74 cm.) l. x 12"h. 10". The two-room doll house has original white-painted frame and exterior, two back-wall windows and an opening door between the rooms. The wall and floor papers are original, and the house is furnished with two early sets: in the bedroom are twin beds, two night stands, and a large armoire of mahogany-finish woods with medallion light-wood inlays; and in the living room is a mahogany-finished ensemble in fine Empire style with gold accents and metallic gold wreath and garland appliques, including tall mirror with shelf, grand buffet, dessert buffet, library table, settee and two chairs. Accessories include parlor stove, potted flowers, curtains with brass rods, bear rug, framed pictures, metal mantel clock, tin baby carriage, various soft-metal pieces including cutlery holder. Four miniature dolls people the

house, including rare bald-head Grandpa. Very good/excellent condition with original papers ad paint having typical play aging. Germany, circa 1900. $1200/1800

286. Wooden Doll Room "The Children's Nursery" by Gottschalk with Wonderful Accessories

25" (64 cm.) l. x 10"h. x 12"d. The wooden room has original ochre and cream painted exterior and facade, original lithographed paper floor to simulate inlay woods, original wall paper with ceiling border, and a constructed set-back area with window. The room is furnished as a nursery with a cream wooden one-piece "wall" having center cloth panel flanked by cupboards on each side, matching twin beds, dressing table, armoire, and small chest with mirror. Additional furnishings include a delightful silk-covered baby bed and matching screen decorated with hand-painted tumbling bears, a high-chair with fancy spindles, and a tiny miniature room, various boxes, and porcelains. A bisque dollhouse mother, and the bisque maid are in the room watching over the little bisque girl who sits in the high chair. Very good condition, some paper wear. The furnishings were made in the workshops of De Petrus Ragout of Netherlands, circa 1890. $1200/1800

287. German Wooden Doll Furnishings and Tea Service
12" (30 cm.) h. screen. Comprising a wooden folding screen, and round table with four chairs in original cream paint with gold accents, along with two silk rose bushes in wooden pots, and with a miniature porcelain tea service with rose and floral design. Excellent condition. Germany, circa 1915, the furniture attributed to Gottschalk. $300/500

288. German Bisque Googly by Gebruder Heubach
9" (23 cm.) Bisque socket head, blue glass side-glancing googly eyes, painted curly lashes, feathered brows, accented nostrils, closed mouth with impish smile, auburn mohair wig, composition five-piece paper mache body, painted white socks and one-strap shoes. Condition: generally excellent. Marks: 95(?) 2/0 Heubach (in square). Comments: Gebruder Heubach, circa 1920. Value Points: rarer googly model with delightful expression, original body, possibly original costume. $500/800

289. German Bisque Googly, 323, by Marseille
9" (23 cm.) Bisque socket head, blue glass sleep and side-glancing googly eyes, painted curly lashes, one-stroke brows, accented nostrils, closed mouth with smug smile, accent line between the lips, brunette mohair wig, five-piece composition body. Condition: generally excellent. Marks: Armand Marseille Germany 323 A 6/0 M. Comments: Marseille, circa 1920. Value Points: fine bisque and expression on the larger model size, with wonderful costume including linen pinafore with embroidery of boys at play. $400/600

290. Fourteen French Postcards of Amusing Googly Dolls

5" (13 cm.) x 3". The tinted-color photographs depict a series of googly dolls in playful poses, circa 1920s, according to postmarks on the reverse. Good condition. $200/300

291. Italian Felt Character Girl by Lenci in Original Costume

13" (33 cm.) Felt swivel head with pressed and painted facial features, blue side-glancing eyes, grey eye shadow, closed mouth, brunette mohair wig, jointing at shoulders and hips, wearing original organdy dress with felt trim, felt coronet of flowers in hair. Condition: generally excellent, museum red ink lettering on back neck, dress a tad dusty with few rents. Comments: Lenci, circa 1930. Value Points: especially expressive features on the wide-eyed girl. $400/500

292. Italian Felt Character Doll by Lenci in Original Costume, with Box

16" (41 cm.) Felt swivel head with pressed and painted facial features, side-glancing brown eyes, grey eye shadow, closed mouth with shaded bottom lip with two accent dots, jointing at shoulders and hips. Condition: generally excellent, slight fading of pink felt, few moth holes at top of hat. Comments: Lenci, circa 1930. Value Points: fine unplayed with condition, the little girl wears her original pink organdy and felt dress with felt bonnet trimmed with a coronet of colorful felt flowers, original undergarments, socks and shoes, and presented in her original colorful Lenci box. $800/1100

293. French Manufacturer's Catalog of Baby Carriages

6" (15 cm.) x 9". The 40 page catalog from Devillaine Freres of Charlieu, France, dated 1931, has photographs, descriptions and price list of their complete line of carriages, strollers, wooden carts, pedal cars, and collapsible leather strollers. Excellent condition. $200/300

294. European Wooden Toy Ferris Wheel and Music Box

14" (36 cm.) h. 11" x 11" base. Arranged upon its original wooden base with painted and lithographed cover to simulate a brick foundation, is a fretwork-carved wooden ferris wheel with four double-sided gondola type chairs, steps leading to the chairs, and a wooden cabinet with etched glass windows that contains the handwind music box. The ferris wheel is arranged to work with a 12 volt transformer (not included). Excellent condition with original colorful finish. Early-20th century, maker unknown, construction and decoration suggest commercial production $700/1100

295. German Wooden Dollhouse Fencing and Flower Patches

2 ½" (6 cm.) h. Thirty-four (34) 5 ½" sections of wooden picket fences are included, with painted gold posts (two posts missing) along with a 16" section with center opening gate. Also included are six 3" diam. heavy card stock circlets designed as little garden patches, with attached moss and flowers. Germany, circa 1920. $200/400

296. Pair, German Bisque Miniature Dolls with Toy Squirrels

5" (13 cm.) Each doll has bisque socket head, glass inset eyes, painted features, closed mouth, brunette mohair wig, five-piece paper mache body, painted shoes and socks, and is wearing aqua flannel coat, cap and muff. Excellent condition. Germany, circa 1915. Included with the little dolls are four miniature squirrels and a hedgehog, three with original German paper labels, along with a carved bone hobby horse with turquoise silk tie. $300/500

297. German Bisque Child with Little Toys
22" (56 cm.) Bisque socket head, brown glass sleep eyes, mohair lashes, painted lashes, open mouth, four teeth, brunette mohair wig, composition and wooden ball-jointed body, wearing her factory original organdy dress and bonnet, shoes and stockings. Condition: generally excellent. Marks: MOA (in star) 200 Welsh

Made in Germany 7 ½. Comments: Max Oskar Arnold for Welsch & Co, circa 1920. Value Points: included with the doll is a wooden bunny coop with little bunnies, along with composition chickens, roosters and a turkey. $300/500

298. An All-Original German Bisque Toddler with Boston Terrier Pup
12" (30 cm.) Bisque socket head, blue glass sleep eyes, painted lashes and brows, open mouth with two porcelain upper teeth, sculpted tongue, blonde mohair wig, composition five piece toddler body with side-hip jointing. Condition: generally excellent, few tears in jacket. Marks: P.M. 914 1. Comments: Porzellanfabrick Mergensgereuth, circa 1920. Value Points: wonderful cheery expression on the chubby dimpled cheeks, original body and body finish, original store costume, and carrying a miniature toy Boston Terrier dog. $500/800

299. Petite German Two-Room Christmas Dollhouse with Fine Original Curtains, Music Room and Musical Piano

22" (56 cm.) l. x 10"h. x 9"d. A petite two room wooden doll house has light brown finish on facade with fancily-carved columns, ochre painted exterior side and back, original wall paper with floor and ceiling borders, and original floor papers to simulate woven carpeting. There are three opening windows at the back, each with original cornice and wonderful original silk draperies with embroidered details. A doorway between the two rooms has lithographed architectural detail on frame and door. The house is furnished with dropfront desk having faux-rosewood finish, two upholstered chairs, unusual upholstered bench, and fernery, while a decorated Chistmas tree stands in the center, and a miniature cardboard nativity scene sits atop the desk. In the smaller room is a large wooden grand piano with hinged keyboard and attached music sheets, whose top is covered with decorative miniature frames, statuary, and rare silver four-arm candelabrum. The piano is musical (keywind on underside) which plays Silent Night when the lid is lifted. A dollhouse bisque woman and dog are in the parlor. Excellent condition. Germany, circa 1910, wonderful original details and charming themes in the appealing smaller-size rooms. $1200/1700

300. Collection of Children's Toys and Candy Cones

2" (5 cm.) cones. Including 8 crepe paper and paper lace candy cones designed for children on their first day of school. Along with a box of miniature six-sided puzzles, a tiny all-bisque doll in her original box labeled "May All Your Troubles be Little Ones", harmonica, carved bone hobby horse, bag of marbles and two rare clear sulphur marbles with camel and bear. Excellent condition. Germany, early-20th century. $200/400

301. Collection of Cards Depicting Children with Dolls and Toys

4" (10 cm.) x 6" largest. More than 50 cards including trade cards, postcards, scrapbook images and others depicting children at play with dolls. Good/excellent condition. Late-19th/early-20th century. $200/400

302. Small German Wooden School Room with Eight Students

14" (36 cm.) l. x 7"h. x 7"d. The wooden one-room school house has original wall and floor papers and original wooden school benches, teacher's desk, tabled easel with slate, bookcase. Eight all0bisque students sit at the school benches, each with a personal slate, abacus, leather school bag, and pencil, and on the nearby bookcases are miniature paper journals for each. Excellent condition, maps are not original. Germany, attributed to Gottschalk, circa 1900, rare tiny size with wonderful accessories. $800/1200

303. Large Collection of Vintage Christmas Ornaments

13" (33 cm.) largest tree. Comprising three vintage Christmas trees with wooden bases and various glass and candle ornaments, paper mache St. Nicholas figure with flocked coat (base lid missing), a wonderful set of paper mache Nativity figures in original cardboard box, lot of miniature Christmas tree ornaments in old box with illustrated lid, and four various hanging ornaments. Very good/excellent condition. Germany, early-20th century. $800/1100

304. English Soft Paste Staffordshire Dishes with Childhood Themes

4 ½" (11 cm.) h. largest tureen. The soft paste creamy service features transfer scenes of childhood nursery rhymes and stories, as well as scenes of children at play, comprising large lidded tureen, two small lidded tureens, footed bowl, two footed compotes, two sauce dishes with attached under-plates, two serving dishes, pickle dish, tiny covered jar, small oval serving dish, six soup bowls and six plates. Excellent condition, few small chips. English, Staffordshire, circa 1880, wonderful images in beautiful blue colors. $300/500

304.1. German Lithographed-Tin Bathroom by Maerklin

11" (28 cm.) h. x 17"l. x 9"d. The heavy-tin bathroom has original cream painted finish with lithographed tile designs on the walls and floor, with built-out compartment as water receptacle that leads into the ceramic bathtub and sink, each with original metal faucets and plugs on chains; additionally there is a pull-chain shower, metal-framed mirror, two attached metal towel bars and radiator. The room has the Maerklin stamp at the side. Excellent condition. Germany, Maerklin, circa 1910. $1200/1800

304.2. Collection of German Tin Dollhouse Accessories, Probably Maerklin

9 ½" (24 cm.) cabinet. Each is of tin with painted finish, including bathroom double sink with mirror, water receptacle at the back, working faucets and plugs, and with matching bucket; along with three parlor stoves of different designs (stove with bird motif has few paint flakes and missing cap), and a rare kitchen bread box with gold stencil. Very good/excellent. Germany, circa 1890/1910, attributed to Maerklin. $800/1200

305. Large German Wooden Well-Stocked Kitchen
40" (102 cm.) l. x 20"h. x 20"d. The large wooden kitchen has back-wall window with multi-panes, built-in cabinets with shelves and drawers, matching work table, chair, bench and sink, and a tin stove with brass oven doors and claw feet. The kitchen has original white finish with architectural columns at the front, and green painted foundation and interior walls, brown painted floor. The kitchen is well supplied and fitted, with numerous pieces of kitchenware, porcelain canisters and dishes, coffee grinder, rare asparagus dish with figural design, rare sausage dish with figural design, enamel ware, earthenware molds, collection of copper pudding molds, and more. A paper mache doll with glass eyes presides over the kitchen. Very good condition. Germany, circa 1890. $1500/2100

306. Fine German Two Room Furnished "Christmas and Butterfly" Dollhouse by Gottschalk

32" (81 cm.) l. x 13"h. x 14"d. The two room dollhouse has original cream-painted facade with gold accented columns, gray painted exterior, and original wall and floor papers in the interior. A double door with rich paneling and Gottschalk silver handle on the parlor side opens between the rooms. The larger room has two back-wall windows with brass rods and lace curtains, and is furnished with a Gottschalk parlor set having mahogany-like finish with gold accents, comprising luxury one-piece settee set in wooden frame with mirror and cabinets, table, two upholstered arm chairs, jardiniere; the matching dessert buffet, matching silk upholstered settee and chair and several small tables are in the adjoining Christmas-themed room. Accessories include two ceramic parlor stoves, soft metal gilt jardiniere with potted flowers, mantel clocks, glassware, ormolu accessories, and, a rare framed shadowbox of miniature butterflies that hangs on the wall. A decorated Christmas tree centers the smaller room along with a miniature holiday-decorated house, a nativity scene, and a bounty of Christmas toys including Erzebirge wooden toys, dolls, spinning top and more. A fine gilt-metal framed print hangs on the back wall, and there are other prints and mirrors. Three small bisque children play in the Christmas room along with their Papa, while in the parlor are three dollhouse adults. Very good played with condition, parlor wall paper and Christmas room floor papers are especially attractive. Germany, circa 1890 $2000/3000

#306 detail

#306 detail

307. French Porcelain Dinner Service with Rare Serving Dishes
5" (13 cm.) h. footed serving dish. Of fine white porcelain with gold bands and pencil striping, the service comprises a rare lidded tureen on high footed pedestal, a larger lidded tureen, two small double-handled lidded serving dishes, gravy boat with under-dish, two leaf-shaped relish dishes, large footed bowl, three smaller footed bowls, oval platter, round platter, 15 various shallow soup bowls or dinner plates, along with a pair of glass candle holders. Excellent condition. French, circa 1880. $400/600

308. Thirty French Etrennes Postcards Featuring Children with Dolls
5" (13 cm.) x 3". The heavy card stock postcards each feature a photographic image of children playing with dolls and toys, presumably just received as their Etrennes Christmas holiday gifts. Very good/excellent condition. Late-19th/early-20th century. $200/400

309. German Bisque Toddler, 680, by Kley and Hahn with Christmas Tree and Snowman Candy Container
14" (36 cm.) Bisque socket head, blue glass sleep eyes, painted lashes and feathered brows, accented nostrils, brunette mohair bobbed wig, composition and wooden ball-jointed toddler body with side-hip jointing, wearing antique flannel jacket with cutwork collar and cuffs, flannel breeches, striped stockings, black buckle shoes. Condition: generally excellent. Marks: 680 K&H made in Germany. Comments: Kley and Hahn, circa 1915. Value Points: wonderful expression, original wig, toddler body, body finish, antique costume, and owning his own German snow man candy container and miniature Christmas tree with candles and glass balls. $800/1100

310. French Wooden Buffet with Porcelains
20" (51 cm.) The dark stained buffet has a fitted cabinet base whose doors have oval glass medallions and two silverware drawers. The shelved top features fancy spindles supporting graduated-size curved front shelves and there is a surmounting crest at the top. Nine 19th century miniature porcelains decorate the shelves. Excellent condition. French, circa 1890. $500/800

311. French Porcelain Doll's Dinner Service and Cutlery
5 ½" (14 cm.) h. tureen. Of fine white porcelain with acorn-shaped finials on lids, decorated with pale green borders and gold pencil stripes, the service includes footed lidded tureen, two footed compotes, two sauce dishes with attached under-trays, large bowl, two oval platters, large service dish, shallow footed bowl, two relish dishes, six soup bowls, and 11 dinner plates. Along with a pewter cutlery service for six including 5 ½" bone-handled knives, spoons and forks, in original red lined box. And with a bisque lobster figural box. Excellent condition, few tiny chips. French, circa 1880. $400/600

312. Fine French Miniature Glass Service, Napoleon III
7" (18 cm.) h. decanter. Of very fine quality blown glass, the remarkably-complete service includes two decanters with stoppers, two additional water decanters, and 23 various stemware for red wine or liquers. There are four different sizes/shapes of glasses (one size lacking one glass), suggesting the complete service for different courses of a banquet. Excellent condition, very rare to find such a large and complete service. French, circa 1870. $300/600

313. Three Miniature Framed Engravings
5" (13 cm.) x 3 ½" gold frames. Comprising a pair of engravings in gold frames, each signed Dupreel, one depicting a man holding a basket of toys for which three young lads are eagerly clamoring; along with a carved wooden frame with print depicting aristocratic lady and gentleman strolling with dog. Excellent condition. 19th century. $300/500

314. French Miniature Porcelain Tea Service in Original Box
8" (20 cm.) x 7" box. A heavy card stock box with hinged lid held by green silk ribbons, opens to reveal fitted interior with white porcelain tea service trimmed with gold edging and black handles and unusual dainty feet which appear even on the little cups. Along with six gold spoons, a sugar tong, and folded napkins. Excellent condition of contents, box a bit worn on exterior. French, circa 1885. $500/700

315. Very Fine French Wooden Doll Bed with Silk Curtains
20" (51 cm.) h. x 13"w. x 19"d. Of finely-grained dark walnut, the doll bed features fancily-spindled footboard posts with decorative bronze garland on the footboard, and a high canopy top attached to the headboard with finial drop decorations. The bed has original slats, mattress, and wonderful old bed fittings highlighted by dark green silk curtains and bed covering trimmed with mauve velvet. Excellent condition. French, circa 1875. $900/1500

316. Petite French Bisque Poupée, Size B, by Leon Casimir Bru

12" (30 cm.) Bisque swivel head on kid-edged bisque shoulder plate, blue glass enamel inset eyes, dark eyeliner, delicately-painted lashes and brows, accented nostrils, closed mouth with slightly upturned lip corners lending a hint of smile, blonde mohair wig over cork pate, kid gusset-jointed body with stitched and separated fingers, wearing antique ivory silk costume, undergarments, slippers, bonnet. Condition: generally excellent. Marks: B (head and shoulders). Comments: Leon Casimir Bru, circa 1870, his deposed model believed to be a portrait of Empress Eugenie. Value Points: beautiful model with lovely bisque and painting, rare petite size with original wig and body. $2200/2800

317. French Doll's Tufted Chair and Fur Dog

8" (20 cm.) chair. 5"l. dog. The wooden-framed chair is upholstered in pale pink muslin printed with tiny roses, having deep tufting on seat and back with self-covered buttons, pleated skirt. Along with a paper mache white fur covered dog with amber glass eyes and open mouth. Excellent condition. French, circa 1910. $300/500

318. French Porcelain Doll's Dinner Service and Cutlery in Original Box

5" (13 cm.) Of fine white porcelain with rich pink bands and gold and black pencil-striped edging, the service comprises a lidded footed tureen, double-handled sauce dish with attached under-tray, covered sauce dish with attached under-tray, 24 various plates and bowls, and footed compote. Along with a set of pewter cutlery for six, in its original sateen-lined box, comprising bone-handled knives, forks and spoons, and a serving spoon. Excellent condition. French, circa 1880. $300/600

319. Art Nouveau Tall Clock with Cherubic Mount

13" (33 cm.) The tall case clock with wooden frame and bronze facade is highly-stylized Art Nouveau with flowing flowers and scrolls and surmounted by a winged cherub, celluloid clock face with intertwined TH (?) letters, with drop pendulums and weight. Case excellent, clock not working. A beautiful case with richly-designed Art Nouveau themes. $300/500

320. French Wooden Toilette Table with Accessories

15" (38 cm.) The walnut-finished wooden toilette table has white marble top and oval mirror that hinges between two fancily-carved bracket poles, ball-spindle legs, two towel bars. Included is a porcelain wash bowl and pitcher set with jars along with rose sateen powder puff with bone tip. Excellent condition. French, circa 1880. $300/500

321. Beautiful French Bisque Poupée by Jumeau with Silk Costume

17" (43 cm.) Bisque swivel head on kid-lined bisque shoulder plate, blue glass enamel inset eyes, dark eyeliner, painted lashes, feathered brows, rose-blushed eye shadow, accented nostrils, closed mouth with accented lips, pierced ears, blonde mohair wig over cork pate, kid gusset-jointed body with shapely torso, stitched and separated fingers. Condition: generally excellent. Marks: 4 (head and shoulders). Comments: Pierre-Francois Jumeau, circa 1870, included with the doll are her antique undergarments and lovely ivory and gold silk gown with pearl trim. Value Points: very beautiful poupée with original wig having original coiffure with waist-lenth curls and very sturdy original body. $2500/3500

322. French Porcelain Dinner Service in Original Box

15" (38 cm.) x 10" box. A wooden storage box with original flower-patterned fabric cover has three layers of doll-sized dinner service inside, including 22 various plates, 4 lidded footed tureens, bowls, two footed compotes, and a variety of relish dishes and other serving pieces, along with various glassware including 6 stem-ware glasses, two water carafes, two amber decanters, and various other amenities of a fine dining table. The set is incomplete, and has a few damages, but is a wonderful example of luxury toy of late-19th century. French, circa 1890. $300/500

#323

#324 closed

#324 open

323. French Porcelain-de-Paris Dainty Dinner Service

3 ½" (9 cm.) h. tureen. Of fine white porcelain decorated with very dainty pink flowers with green leaves and gilt garlands, the service comprises a lidded tureen, a larger footed tureen, four various footed compotes, lidded casserole dish with under-tray, sauce dish with under-tray, two oval platters, two large rounded plates, 21 dinner and dessert plates, two footed dessert plates. Excellent condition. French, circa 1880. $400/600

#325

324. French Wooden Doll's Salon Cabinet with Gold Leaf Finish

19" (48 cm.) The wooden cabinet in the Louis XVI style has gracefully-curved legs with acanthus carving, bottom shelf and center drawer with gilt metal pulls, with upper cabinet having bombe-shaped doors and curved roof, the gold leaf decorated with painted blue medallions and floral clusters, along with a key for the cabinet doors. Excellent condition. French, circa 1875. $300/500

325. Splendid French Porcelain Doll's Dinner Service with Rare Pieces

6" (15 cm.) Of fine white porcelain with deep rose borders edged with gold leaf and having gold-leaf accented acorn and leaf finials on lids, the service comprises a footed lidded tureen, two lidded casserole dishes, five various footed compotes, double-handled sauce dish with attached under-tray, small sauce tureen with lid and ladle, large bowl, oval platter, large serving dish, eight soup bowls, eight dinner plates, five saucers, four cups (one handle reglued), coffee pot with lid, lidded sugar and creamer and a footed fruit bowl, each service piece with gold lettered monogram "A.B." indicating its exclusive commissioned production, very rare to find monograms on child-sized set. Excellent condition except as noted. French, circa 1870. $500/800

#326

326. French Porcelain Doll's Dessert Service

4" (10 cm.) Of fine white porcelain with rich gold-leaf decorations and borders, the service comprises lidded coffee pot, lidded sugar, creamer, four cups and saucers, and a dessert bowl. Excellent condition. French, circa 1880. $300/500

327. Mlle Emilie Bonnarilet's French Miniature Dollhouse Furnishings in Original Box

14" (36 cm.) l. x 8" (assembled) x 10"d. Sold in this original box which is designed to serve as room walls and floor, the one-room salon has two glass windows with original pink satin curtains and lace inserts, original printed wall-paper with faux-wood grain wainscoting, fireplace with rose sateen cover and attached clock shelf, and matching mahogany-finished furniture including upright piano, jardiniere with moss and flowers, turtle-top parlor table, settee and four matching chairs with rose sateen upholstery. Along with an ormolu plant stand, two other potted flowers, clock (missing paper face) with figural lady at the crest, two silver candlesticks, two matching paper-framed mirrors and a paper framed print. Good condition, with fading, age wear, box worn. French, circa 1875, the box lid bears the hand-written name of the original child owner, Mlle Emilie Bonnarilet. $1000/1600

328. French Candy Container in the Shape of Boulle Chest, with Equestrian Statue

7 ½" (19 cm.) h. 8"w. A heavy card stock candy box is in the shape of 18th century Boulle-style French cabinet with lithographed paper cover to simulate rich inlays and bronze mounts; the two drawers originally held candies from a luxury Paris candy shop and the chest was laster used as furniture in a doll world. Along with a gilded metal miniature stature of horses. Excellent condition. French, circa 1880. $400/600

329. 19th Century Doll-Sized Table Accessories

4" (10 cm.) l. tray. Comprising a fine hallmarked silver tray with repousse designs and beaded edging, tall clear glass blown pitcher with rich pattern, two footed compotes with pressed patterns, and a bronze or cast brass bust of a woman with costume and jewelry details. Excellent condition. Mid/late-19th century. $300/500

330. French Wooden Doll's Salon Cabinet with Gold Leaf Finish

19" (48 cm.) The wooden cabinet in the Louis XVI style has gracefully-curved legs with acanthus carving, bottom shelf and center drawer with gilt metal pulls, with upper cabinet having bombe-shaped doors and curved roof, the gold leaf decorated with painted blue medallions and floral clusters, along with key for the cabinet doors. Excellent condition. French, circa 1875. $300/500

331. Collection of Very Fine 19th Century Doll-Sized Glass

3 ½" (9 cm.) yellow vase. Including a blown glass yellow vase with ruffled edge, two-piece glass epergne with gold edging and beaded design; turquoise blue bud vase with gild trim, opaque-green glass vase with floral painted designs, fine cut glass vase, and a rare etched cameo glass dish on scrolled brass frame, signed Touchard. Excellent condition. Late-19th century. $600/1000

332. 19th Century Doll's Recamier with Original Tufted Upholstery

17" (43 cm.) l. The wooden framed recamier rests upon ball-shaped feet and has original (frail) purple silk upholstery that is very deeply-tufted with black bead buttons, black silk sides, and rich mauve, cream and brown braided cording along the seams. French, circa 1870, a very beautiful piece of furniture with rich and rare colors. $400/600

333. Fine Maitrise Quality Chest of Drawers with Floral and Bird Inlays

10" (25 cm.) h. x 11"w. The finely-crafted rosewood, doll-sized chest of drawers is constructed with shaped top, curved drawer fronts, and angled side supports that form into shapely legs, and has rich inlays and etched designs including lovebirds, scrolls, vases of flowers, lion, violin, and is signed with the etched initials J.B. Excellent condition. $700/1200

336. French Art Nouveau Fruitwood Armoire

19" (48 cm.) Of fine fruitwood with natural light finish, the highly-stylized Art Nouveau armoire has carved floral crest, richly scrolled cornice, and mahogany panels to offer contrast. There are two full-length mirrored closet doors above two lower drawers, and the narrow center cabinet has four small jewelry drawers. Each of the drawers has original rose sateen lining. Excellent condition. French, circa 1890. $400/600

334. English Burled Walnut Cabinet in Unusual Narrow Shape

17" (43 cm.) The narrow cabinet of finely-grained woods with inlay burled borders and pencil stripes, and having a glass-front upper cabinet with lattice-work panels. Excellent condition, one small piece of word veneer missing on foot. English, late-19th century. $500/800

335. French Maitrise Wooden Chest of Drawers with Marble Top

9" (23 cm.) h. 12"w. 6"d. The wooden two-drawer chest with dove-tailed construction and of finest quality wood veneers to enhance wood graining and inlays, has bombe shaped front and sides, carved apron, bronze mounts and draw pulls and rose marble top. Excellent condition. French, mid-19th century, of maitrise quality. $700/1100

337. 19th Century Tilt-Top Doll's Table with Chippendale-Style Chair

8" (20 cm.) h. table. 12" table tilted. Comprising a 12-sided table with elaborately-inlaid design of wood top, on a three-leg pedestal base; the table can be tilted for placement against a wall when not in use. Along with a walnut-finish Chippendale style chair with beautifully-shaped back and legs, velvet seat. Excellent condition. $400/600

338. French Bisque Poupée Attributed to Jumeau

14" (36 cm.) Bisque swivel head on kid-edged bisque shoulder plate, blue glass enamel inset eyes, dark eyeliner, painted lashes and brows, closed mouth with accented lips, pierced ears, blonde mohair wig over cork pate, kid gusset-jointed body with stitched and separated fingers, antique costume. Condition: bisque excellent, body has mends, hands fragile. Comments: Emile Jumeau, circa 1875. Value Points: beautiful face with lovely bisque and painting. $1600/2100

339. Antique Costume and Accessories for Bébé
Featuring an ivory satin quilted coat with lush mohair collar and lace trim, for bébé about 18"-20". Along with 3" ankle boots, mohair collar and muff, smaller lambswool muff, and a leather purse (unsigned, but other examples are known with Bébé Jumeau or Au Nain Bleu stamp on interior kid lining). Very good condition, circa 1900. $300/500

340. German Miniature Glassware in Original Box
6" (15 cm.) x 4" box. 1 ¼" objects. A 12-compartment cardboard box holds 12 decorative blown glass objects for dollhouse use, including candlesticks, oil lamp, birdcage. Excellent condition, factory original. Germany, circa 1930. $100/200

#341

#342

341. German Doll-Size Glassware and Table Accessories
3" (8 cm.) compote. Comprising a fine crystal compote with unusual fluted rim, a lemonade pitcher with colorful enamel designs and with matching cookie jar and two glasses, a green glass pitcher with enamel designs, and a pair of pewter candlesticks. Excellent condition. Early-20th century. $300/500

342. German Doll-Sized Accessories for Table Settings
2 ½" (6 cm.) pitcher. Sized for display with 15"-16" lady doll, or smaller child

- 156 -

doll, comprising a wonderful porcelain tea set with floral-shaped handles and matching leaf-shaped tray; along with a clear glass pitcher decorated with black bands and green beading and having 9 matching glasses, and with another clear-glass pitcher with enamel decorations and 2 matching glasses, and an embroidered silk tea cozy. Excellent condition. Circa 1900. $400/700

343. German Woven Carriage with All-Bisque Baby

8" (20 cm.) carriage. 5" doll. The woven wicker carriage has original leather sunshade and wooden hand drip, with iron frame and spoked wheels. Along with an all-bisque baby with pink-tinted bisque, painted hair and facial features, jointed limbs, antique knit costume. Excellent condition. Germany, early-20th century. $400/600

344. Two German Doll-Sized Decorated Christmas Trees and Decorated Stand

13" (33 cm.) and 8" tree. Two vintage Christmas trees with wooden tree stands are decorated with glass balls and candle decorations. Included is a 6"l. wooden pine platform with colorful folk art painted decorations. Excellent condition. Early-20th century. $400/600

345. Sonneberg Bisque Doll in the Look-Alike French Manner, with Original Costume

16" (41 cm.) Bisque socket head, large blue glass eyes, dark eyeliner, delicately painted lashes and brows, accented eye corners and nostrils, closed mouth with outlined lips, blonde mohair wig, Sonneberg composition and wooden fully-jointed body with straight wrists. Condition: generally excellent. Marks: 8. Comments: Sonneberg, circa 1882, the doll was aimed at capturing the favored French doll market, and closely resembles early bébés of

Jumeau. Value Points: beautiful doll with lovely painting, wearing her original maroon silk dress with brown velvet detailing, undergarments, black knit stockings, brown kidskin shoes, and brown felt flannel bonnet with maroon and brown velvet silk trim. $1100/1500

346. Extensive Netherlands Soft-Paste Child's Dinner Service, and Menu Cards

6" (15 cm.) h. largest tureen. Of creamy soft-paste with lavish flowing blue floral decorations, the child or doll-sized dinner service comprises lidded footed tureen, two oval lidded casseroles, two gravy boats with attached under-tray, unusual relish dish with pitcher center, scallop-edge footed compote, pair of two small covered dishes with under-trays, large bowl with drain dish, six oval platters, two relish dishes, five oval platters, four round serving plates, seventeen various plates or soup bowls, two fruit bowls, and two ladles. Excellent condition except repair to ladles. Each piece has blue stamp "Parseme No3" and is attributed to Petrus Regout of Maastricht, Netherlands, circa 1890. Along with 12 menu cards with hand-written menus for lavish banquets, 1890 era. $300/600

347. Cream Wool Twill Dress for Lady Doll

To fit lady doll about 20". Of fine cream wool twill the shapely dress has coat sleeves, and is decorated with blue cord braid and a blue silk sash that extends around the hips. Very good condition, some minor fabric wear. Included is mannequin stand. Circa 1870. $300/500

348. Decorative Accessories for Doll's Furnishings

5" (13 cm.) statue. Including a fine porcelain figure of Cupid with wings and bow, on pedestal (one finger tip chipped) with original Dresden stamp; pair of 3" French porcelain vases with floral decorations; and soft-paste wash bowl and pitcher with matching chamber pot and bowl, each with blue background and hand-painted blue bird theme, ink-marked "R". Excellent condition except as noted. Late-19th century. $300/500

349. Mahogany Doll-Sized Buffet with Elaborate Shelving

17" (43 cm.) The diminutive-sized doll furniture, perfectly scaled to display with 10"-12" lady dolls, is constructed with elaborate shelving, four different mirrors, silverware drawers and glass front lower cabinet. Very good condition with fine original finish. $300/500

350. Two German Vintage Christmas Trees

11" (28 cm.) Each perched on wooden tree base, and each is decorated with white and silver Christmas balls and candles. Very good condition. Germany, early-20th century. $400/600

351. Petite French Bisque Poupée by Jumeau, Size 1, with Original Signed Body

10" (25 cm.) Bisque swivel head on kid-edged bisque shoulder plate, blue glass paperweight inset eyes, dark eyeliner, painted lashes and brows, accented nostrils, closed mouth with accented lips, pierced ears, blonde mohair wig with original interwoven ribbons and hip-length braids, shapely kid poupée body with tiny waist, gusset-jointed hips, stitched and separated fingers, and wearing original muslin chemise. Condition: generally excellent, body especially sturdy. Marks: 1 (head and shoulders) Jumeau Medaille d'Or Paris (body). Comments: Emile Jumeau, circa 1880. Value Points: sought-after petite size 1 poupée has wonderful original wig, original earrings, sturdy signed original body. $1100/1700

352. English Wooden Hall Table and Porcelain Dishes

5" (13 cm.) The demi-lune shaped hall table has fine Hepplewhite style shape, with burled veneer wood inlay designs, and included are six miniature porcelain plates (one signed Limoges), a partial signed Limoges coffee service, and a wash bowl and pitcher set signed Limoges. Excellent condition. Late-19th century. $300/500

354. Miniature Porcelain and Glass Accessories

2" (5 cm.) h. Chinese vases. Including a pair of blue and white Chinese ceramic vases; a porcelain coffee service with silver lustre finish, and having maker's mark, comprising tray, coffee pot with lid, sugar with lid, creamer and one cup and saucer; Chinese cloisonne urn with lid and two matching vases; glass water carafe and tumbler; three various Limoges vases; and a miniature Limoges porcelain tea set with blue flowers on yellow background. Excellent condition, Late-19th century. $300/500

355. Accessories and Ephermera for Bébés or Larger Poupées

18" (46 cm.) l. parasol. Including a wooden-handled folding parasol with bone tip and silk plaid cover; velvet and straw bonnet; fox-tail fur collar; three 1920s hat boxes with hats; lady's corset; blue beaded bag; two rare wooden candy boxes in the shape of doll trunks; blue beaded bag, cardboard trunk whose steamer label reads "Durch Filboten! Bote Bexzahlt" and contains within a paper mache stork with baby. Excellent condition. Late-19/early-20th century. $300/500

356. Accessories and Ephemera for Small Bébés

5" (13 cm.) l. tray. Comprising a richly-gilded oval tray with filigree sides, double-handles, and lace-under-glass surface; tambourine with bells and painted bird scene; gilt metal square hand mirror with enamel flowers; and silk-lined velvet folio with set of gilt-accented soft metal cutlery. Late-19th century. Excellent condition. $300/500

357. French Doll's Wooden Drop Leaf Table with Tea Service

7" (18 cm.) h. table. The wooden table with rich mahogany finish has spindled legs and demi-lune drop leaves which, when raised, changes the table shape to a perfect round. Along with a French porcelain tea service with blue edging and gold striping, comprising lidded teapot, lidded sugar, creamer and four cups and saucers. Excellent condition except creamer handle repaired. French, circa 1875, perfectly sized for display with 16"-18" lady doll. $300/500

358. Miniature Signed Oil Painting on Board

5" (13 cm.) x 4" framed. A still-life oil painting on board depicts a gold vase of blue and yellow flowers, a few loose flowers lying on the table in front of the vase. The painting is signed G. Dubouchet and is presented in gesso-finished wooden frame. Possibly Gustave Dubouchet, French, born 1867. Excellent condition. $200/400

359. Wonderful German Wooden Milliner's Shop with Many Accessories and Dolls

12" (30 cm.) h. x 11"w. x 3"d. The wooden store front with original green painted finish trimmed with white stencil has open shelves and cupboards that are filled with bolts of antique fabrics and trim. Arranged on the shelves are two blonde hair china heads with bonnets, and additional accessories include fans, Art Nouveau mirror, opera glasses, frames, wicker boxes of buttons and sewing notions, wonderful early cardboard box in the shape of a trunk, filled with beads and buttons, and a gilt-accented iron hat rack filled with miniature bonnet. Standing alongside is a bisque head doll marked 16/0 with sleep eyes, open mouth, blonde mohair wig, five-piece paper mache

body, painted boots, wearing antique costume, along with her paper mache fur-covered dog. Very good/excellent condition, a wonderful arrangement. Germany, circa 1900 $800/1200

360. German Porcelain Miniature Dishes

2" (5 cm.) h. tureen. Of fine white porcelain with decorative emerald-green edging, and centered roses with garlands of tiny brightly-colored flowers, including lidded tureen, lidded casserole, oval platter, square serving dish, and seven plates. Excellent condition. Probably French, circa 1875. $200/300

361. German Wooden Milliner's Shop

19" (48 cm.) l. x 9"h. x 9"d. The wooden framed shop with two windows on the back wall has original wall and floor papers, and removable wooden shelving (repainted) that is filled with bolts of fabric and trim and various sewing notions including a little box filled with miniature thread spools labeled "Dolly's Little Set of Silks". There is a tin sewing machine, candle holder, frames, miniature hats, and a mannequin. A German black haired china lady stands in attendance. Late-19th century. $800/1100

#362

362. German Wooden Dollhouse Kitchen, 1920s Era

8" (20 cm.) h. cupboard. Of maple wood with natural finish, the kitchen includes cupboard with unusual porcelain spice drawers and pull-out cutting board, work table with removable sink bowl, work table, table, bench and two chairs. Excellent condition. Germany, circa 1920s. $300/500

363. German Bisque Toddler by Gebruder Heubach

7" (18 cm.) Solid domed bisque socket head, painted light brown hair, painted facial features, deep-blue intaglio eyes with white eyedots, closed mouth with downcast lips, composition five-piece body, wearing antique blue knit suit and cap. Condition: generally excellent. Marks: D 7760 Heubach (square) Germany. Comments: Gebruder Heubach, circa 1920. Value Points: brilliant blue eyes are complemented by wonderful antique blue knit suit on the wistful-faced boy. $300/500

#363

364. German Wooden Wall Rack with Porcelain Spice Drawers

7" (18 cm.) The maple wood hanging cabinet with natural finish has ten spice drawers with labels and blue decoration, along with matching hanging salt box, pitcher, creamer and sugar. Excellent condition. Germany, circa 1920. $200/300

#364

365. German Character Doll in Original Costume and Box

7" (18 cm.) Solid domed socket head of composition or terra cotta with light brown complexion and painted facial features, brown eyes, closed mouth, painted hair, five-piece composition body. Condition: generally excellent. Comments: Germany, circa 1925. Value Points: in unplayed with condition in original box, wearing original muslin costume and turban. $300/500

366. French Wooden Toilette Table and Accessories

9" (23 cm.) The wooden toilette table has original pale blue painting with floral garland trim at the arched back-board, and blue, gold and red pencil-striping, towel racks on each side, along with original white porcelain wash bowl and pitcher, with matching pin tray, soap dish, little plate, and chamber-pot and with an added box of mirror and brush lettered "For My Dolly". The table has especially elegant shaping and lines. Excellent condition. French, circa 1885. $400/600

367. German Bisque Pouting Character, 6969, by Gebruder Heubach

12" (30 cm.) Pink-tinted bisque socket head, blue glass sleep eyes, painted lashes and brows, accented nostrils, closed mouth with downcast pouting lips, blonde mohair wig, composition and wooden ball-jointed body, pretty antique dress. Condition: generally excellent. Marks: 6969 Germany 3 (head) (Holz-masse stamp on body). Comments: Gebruder Heubach, circa 1912. Value Points: fine quality of bisque on the wistful-faced child with original stamped body, original body finish. $900/1300

368. German Celluloid Doll in Original Box with Costumes

7" (18 cm.) h. doll. 11" x 16" box. A brightly-designed cardboard box with lace edging contains within an all-celluloid doll with painted features, jointed limbs, blonde mohair bobbed wig, wearing original undergarments, and along with additional costumes comprising cotton pajamas, rayon and felt party dress with matching cap, woven shawl, felt shoes, and comb and mirror. Excellent unplayed with condition, the items have never been removed from their box, small rub on cheek. Germany, circa 1920. $200/400

#366
#367

#368

#365

There comes a time to say farewell.

369. German Bisque Doll as "Alice in Wonderland" with Grandfather Clock
8" (20 cm.) doll. 10" clock. Bisque shoulder head doll with brown glass eyes, painted features, closed mouth, blonde mohair wig, muslin body with bisque lower legs, painted shoes and socks, wearing blue silk dress with embroidered pinafore, undergarments, woven bonnet, marked 41, excellent condition. Along with a tall case clock with porcelain face, and painted scenes of ocean, country side, and windmill (one hand missing, unknown if working). The doll, presented as Alice in Wonderland, was considered a symbol of the De Kleine Wereld Museum, and fittingly closes the auction, along with clock to mark the hour. Circa 1900. $300/500

"As we close our doors, we are comforted with the knowledge that our collection will continue its journey to new homes."

Els Van Houtven, co-founder of De Kleine Wereld Museum